I Have Never Walked Alone

Jack Beaver

NEWMAN SPRINGS PUBLISHING
320 Broad Street
Red Bank, NJ 07701

First originally published by Newman Springs Publishing 2019

ISBN 978-1-64096-930-8 (Paperback)
ISBN 978-1-64096-931-5 (Digital)

Printed in the United States of America

Preface

I HAVE DECIDED TO WRITE this book because of some incidents that have happened to me during my life. I thought they would be interesting to read.

Although I have classified this book as fiction, most incidents are based on my real life experiences. All dates, times, and places have been changed. The names of characters have been changed. Any resemblance to anyone living or dead is purely coincidental.

Introduction

I WILL START BY TELLING you that I came from a family of five children, of which I was the youngest. My father was a short husky man, who was a blacksmith all his life. He died at the age of sixty-one. My mother, who was on the heavy side, came from West Virginia. She died at the age of seventy-eight. Harold, my brother, is the oldest child. He spent four years in the air force during World War II. Robert is next. He spent three years in the navy during World War II. Thelma got married and had four children. She is now a widow. Norman, who is now deceased, was four F for the draft for the Korean conflict.

I grew up in Southwestern Pennsylvania. Upon graduation from high school, I worked full time in a garage for quite some time. I had been saving all the money I could.

My life's dream was to fly. I was saving my money to buy a small airplane. I would frequently visit the small airfields within fifty miles of my home, hoping to find one for sale. My boss, the owner of the garage where I worked, had bought a new car. He only had it a few months when he offered to sell it to me at a very reasonable price. I bought it, and there went my savings. Just a few days later, I found the airplane I had been looking for. It was for sale, and the price was right, but I was now broke. I went to good old dad. I asked him to cosign a note in which I would put my car up for collateral. He did so reluctantly. He said I would probably kill myself in it.

So I got my plane. It was a 1945 Ercoupe no. n2715h. A short time later, I obtained my student license. Then I flew the pants off that plane.

As I sit here thinking about it, a smile breaks across my face. I have many fond memories of that plane. I will mention just a few of them which I think were the most exciting. These are memories that I wouldn't give up for a million dollars; yet, I wouldn't do them for another million dollars.

1

I'LL START WITH MY FIRST cross country trip. I had about fifty hours of solo flying when my brother Harold was a licensed pilot, and he said he would take me on my first trip. We planned to fly to a small town in North Carolina. It was little over three hours flying time away. That meant we would have to refuel somewhere on the way back. Harold made his own flight plan and a map of all the towns and check points along the way. He also marked all the airfield within a few miles of our course. Then he explained it to me like a battle plan until I had it almost memorized.

The weather was the next problem. It had to cooperate. This was going to be a one-day trip, and we wanted to go on a weekend. On Friday, Saturday looked good, but on Saturday, Sunday looked even better. It was a go all the way.

Early Sunday morning, we got to airfield, topped off the tanks, and took off. Going down to North Carolina, we went to ten thousand feet to get a ten mile per hour tail wind in our favor. Everything went smoothly, as we marked off check point after check point on our map as we flew over them.

We flew over a small rice field with long runways and a lot of aircraft parked on the ground. We both remarked at how nice it was laid out. We decided to stop there and refuel on our way home.

We arrived in North Carolina without a hitch. We had lunch and dinner there. We were not able to get gas there because we had landed at a friend's farm rather than an airfield.

We left shortly after dinner, about 4:00 p.m. We climbed to six thousand feet then got on course. Because things had gone so smoothly on the way there, neither of us were paying much attention to the check points. We were in the middle of a conversation when I noticed nothing but mountains and woods below. I asked what time it was and which check points we should be near. At the same time, I glanced at my compass and noticed that we were still on course, so I didn't get alarmed. Harold said that we should be right over one of the check points now, but there was nothing down there but woods. Harold said he would check his watch for the next one. The time came around, and we were still over woods and mountains.

We decided to continue on the same course and see what would come up. We continued on the course for some time but nothing came up. The wing tank gauge was beside me, so I glanced down at it. It showed the wing tanks were nearly empty which meant that we had one-hour flying time.

A little while later, he asked me how much was left in the wing tanks. I looked down at them and saw they are empty. I told him they were bouncing around on one-eighth of a tank, but I knew we were on the nose tank. The gauge for that tank was a float center of windshield. Several minutes later, he asked me about the tanks again. I told him it was bouncing around on empty.

He said, "You're a damn liar. The nose tank is going down."

I said, "Yes, they were empty the first time you asked."

I said that we were going down while we still had the power. I said that we would pick a field, and if something goes wrong, we could go around and try again or find another field. I cut the power and put the plane in a descent. We went to four hundred feet, looking for a nice soft place to land.

We both noticed a field behind what looked like a row of chicken houses. It was nice and flat and plenty long enough to get in and out of. It looked like a hayfield with hay about six inches long. We buzzed it, looking for fences or obstacles that we should avoid. There were none. It looked good. I did a sharp bank to the left and made a ninety degree turn. Then I flew for about half a mile. I then repeated the left turn and flew parallel to the field. Once again, we gave it a good long look, and it still looked good. I flew about one mile past the field and turned ninety degrees to the field approach, when I noticed off the left wing tip, a barn with a wind sock on it.

I quickly gave it a good look. There it was, a J-3 cub sitting in the shadows of the barn—one hundred and eighty degrees to the left. That's when Harold started screaming, "What the hell are you doing?"

I just said, "You'll see." I flew for about half a mile and repeated the turn. Then leveling out of the turn, I cut the power and nosed down. I pointed out the other plane to Harold. The look on his face was one of relief. I had to admit; the first field looked better.

We landed in the field and taxied to the barn where we were met by an angry man about fifty-year-old. He explained that we were not allowed to land there because it was a private field, and that it wasn't on the map. We told him that we were lost and out of gas. We explained that we were in the pattern for the chicken farm when we saw this wind stock and J-3 cub.

We asked where we were.

He said, "You're in Warfield, West Virginia." We checked our map and found that we were sixty miles off course. We couldn't figure out how we had got there. The man had by now introduced himself. He said that a pretty good wind out of the west had blown for about an hour, and they died out.

That was not the end of this exciting trip. The man had no gas. He told us the best he could do was to take one of us in his truck to the local filling station. There we could get a few gallons of Amoco white gas.

Harold went with him. They came back in half an hour with an old rusty five-gallon can full of gas. We left about a gallon in the can because we were afraid of getting dirt out of the bottom of the can.

We asked the man where we could get some more gas. He told us to go up the valley which we were in for about fifteen minutes. He asked where we were going. We told him Pittsburgh, Pennsylvania, was our destination. He said to continue flying up the valley until we came to a Y in the road and a drive-in-theater. We were to land across the road in an unmarked field. We could get gas there.

We thanked him and took off with about thirty or forty minutes of gas. We flew up the valley for fifteen minutes then came to a Y in the valley. The biggest was northeast, away from the way we wanted to go, so we took the smaller one, the one going toward home. After five minutes in the air, we could see no Y in the road. We didn't see a drive-in-theater either.

It was past the point of no return. Harold said, "Let's get above the ridges and see what the hell we can see." While climbing, I noticed it was getting dust, and some cars on the road below were already using parking lights.

We got above the ridges, and out on the horizon was a beacon flashing. I turned a few degrees to line up on it. Neither of us were too excited over it because some of them are markers for airlines. We had one several miles from home like that. It was only a minute or so when Harold started yelling, "Look at those runways." I thought he was seeing things, and then I saw them too. They were hard surface runways, two of them and mighty long.

I told him I was going straight down in without flying the pattern and going down wind. I lined up on the runway and cut the power. Everything was going just fine until I was at fifty feet and clearing the fences at the end of runway. Harold started to yell and pointed to the other end of the runway. I looked up and saw a DC-3 in the exact same position we were, at the other end of the runway. I said, "The hell with him, as soon as I get all three wheels on the ground. I'll run it into the grass." The DC-3 put on the power and went around again.

We thought we were in trouble. While taxing toward the tower and fuel pumps, we went past the DC-3, and the pilot and the co-pilot glared at us. Past the tower, three well-dressed men came out and looked at us with their hands on hips. One of them followed us to the gas pump.

I got out before he came up. Before he could say anything to me, I said, "Fill it up." He didn't say anything to me instead he just got the pump and filled my wing tanks. He started to hang it back when I said, "Hey, you got another one here." I reached up and took the cap off the nose tank, which he filled.

The plane could hold a total of twenty-three gallons. He put in twenty-two and eight tenths gallons in it. He turned to me and said, "Boy she was nearly dry wasn't she?"

I said, "I didn't think I had enough to fly the pattern." That was all that was said. He walked back to the other two men, the pilot and the co-pilot, and he walked away. I have never heard anything else about that incident.

On several occasions, my girl, Dolores Moore, went to the airfield with me. Each time, I would ask her to go for a ride with me, but she always refused. One day, I told her if she didn't go, I wouldn't go. It was a no go. I got in the plane and asked her to get in. After a little coaxing, she did. I explained the seat belts and showed her how they worked by fastening hers around her. She tried to unbuckle it and couldn't. I took advantage of it and reached up and turned on the switch and hit the starter.

The plane started instantly. I started to taxi to the runway. She didn't say much, just looked petrified. I turned on the runway and took off. I gave her about a one-hour ride. Nice and smooth with no sharp turns, fast descents, or climbs. It was just a nice smooth ride. I then returned to the field. I asked her how she had liked it. She wouldn't answer me, but I got her up several more times without begging her.

I am not telling you these incidents in the order they happened, just as they pop into my head.

One day before going to the field, I asked Harold to show me how to do some stunts. I climbed to four thousand feet. The power on stalls was easy. I was doing them in a series in no time. Then I tried power off, but they were the same. I tried three twenties. I soon caught onto them. They were easy too. The spiral was almost fatal, but I figured it out and tried again. It was okay.

After doing these for a while, I got the bright idea to go over my home and show off. I did, and when I got home, Harold was waiting. I still remember his words. He said, "You damn fool. You'll kill yourself, and I will be to blame. Dad blames me for talking you into getting the plane." Which he didn't do, I did that all on my own. That wasn't the last time I was to hear those words.

I went on third shift. Quitting time was 7:15 a.m. I would leave work and go flying. Then I would go home and sleep for the rest of the day. One day while flying over my home, I thought I would go back to the field, go home, and go to bed. Then I had the bright idea, "Why go to the field, I'm already home." So I landed behind the house in a small field. I knew I would have trouble getting out of it. I parked the plane in front of my dad's two car garage and went to bed. The next thing I knew, my dad was shaking me and saying, "Get that thing the hell out of my driveway." He left the room and in came Harold. I heard those same words again. I went out and moved it. Then Harold explained to me how to get out. I disagreed. He wanted me to go into a mild wind. He said that way was much shorter. After a mild argument, I decided to do it his way. I think to this day he was wrong. Getting out, I went through some small tree tops under some telephone lines, and the plane suffered some damages.

One day while leaving work, three men I worked with decided to go golfing before going home. I told them I would be over the golf course before them, and I would run them off it. They laughed at me and said that if I followed them, I would get a golf club through my windshield. My brother Norman was with me. He asked if I was going to the golf course. I told him that I was, and he wanted to go too.

We went out to the field about five miles away. It was about the same distance as the golf club in the other direction. We took off and flew straight to the golf course. We circled it for a few minutes, and I said, "They must have changed their minds." I started to leave.

Norman looked over his shoulder after a minute or two and said, "Someone is out there now." I was a few miles from the course. I made a wide circle giving them enough time to get well out on number one green. I came into the green like I was landing only with full power. They were right in the middle of it I knew my wheels were only two or three feet from touching the ground. I flew right at them. All this time, Norman was sitting there with his hands on his lap. He yelled and made motion with his hands to get it up.

Another time, it was deer season, and my two brothers and I were planning a day of hunting. Norman and Bob were to wait for me to get home from work, which would make them quite late to get started hunting. My brother Harold didn't hunt. I got home from work to find they had left without me.

The place we planned to hunt was about thirty miles from home in a flood control area. A place called the lope. It had got its name because the river made a huge U shape. It had a deserted railroad which ran across the mouth of the U. It had to be moved because of the flood control project. There were two railroad bridges across the river. They were old-stone arch type about one mile apart.

I tried to make up my mind whether to go and try to find them or not. That wasn't the only area we hunted in the flood control area. I thought about it for a while. I decided to fly up and find them and give them a good buzzing. I knew they would appreciate this about as much as I appreciated them leaving without me. A good buzzing would spook all the game for about a mile around them.

I went to the field and took off. I went straight for the lope. I flew over back and forth looking for them. You couldn't miss Norman; he wore a bright yellow hunter suit. At the time, I think it was the only one in the woods. Everyone else wore red.

I couldn't find them, not even in the parked car. I left the lope flying straight up the center of it. After flying over the railroad for several minutes, I decided to give it one more try.

I turned onto the river and dropped down to about twice as high as the trees following the river. I turned with the river. I had to rise up to go over them. Then I thought the hell with them; I went with full power and followed the river around the lope. Coming out the other side, I saw there was a second bridge with more hunters on it. This one was easier than the first one. The river went straight for a mile and out through some flat lands. I went under this one, too, and then returned home. That evening I found out that they hadn't even gone there. They went to the place we hunted about thirty miles away. I don't think my family knows to this day that I pulled this stunt. I kept quiet about it and hoped that none of those hunters knew me. I didn't want to hear those words again.

Another time, I was flying local when I noticed that I was flying over my foreman's house. He was having a cookout in his backyard. He had a few people there. The house was in the country with large flat hayfields bordering his backyard. It was lined with tall thin trees on one end.

I made a long approach to it. I went across about six hundred feet above it. With full power at one hundred and twenty miles per hour, I flew straight toward the trees. At the last instant, I put the plane in a vertical climb until the airspeed said sixty-five, and the altimeter said three hundred feet. I leveled off and left instantly because there was a big highway close by.

My foreman never said anything to me about it until one day, four or five years later, after I had gotten rid of the plane. I was walking out of the plant one day when someone nudged me in the ribs. I turned around, and it was my old foreman. He said in a low voice, "Tell me the truth. You were watching us down in the yard and didn't notice how close you were to the trees, weren't you?"

I said, "I didn't even see you or anyone else once I got close to the ground. I was watching the trees and airspeed and went right up the side of them."

He said, "You're not kidding. You went right up the side of them." He told me about five minutes after I was gone; they were still blowing back and forth. He also told me that a state police stopped and wanted to know if we knew the owner of the plane. He told them that he'd never seen it before.

While on third shift, a fellow worker and I became good friends. His name was Kenny. He was about five years older than me, and he was married. He lived on a farm about five miles out of town. I flew over his farm several times but never saw anyone around. One morning while flying over his farm, I noticed two men cutting corn and making corn stocks like you would see in a Halloween advertisement. I buzzed it at about fifty feet and wobbled the ailerons. One of the men waved a corn knife at me. I said to myself, "You'll be sorry for that." The next pass I came down across the field right at them. I could hear the corn hitting my wheels. One man ran and hid behind a corn stock. The other ran for the nearby woods. I left immediately. That night, I was going to tease him about it. When I told him about it, I asked him why he had run. He started to laugh like hell. When he had settled down, I asked him what was so funny. He said, "That field belongs to my neighbor."

Well, that's enough of my stunts. I could go out with a few more, but I won't. I will continue on with the story. A close friend, which I will not name, and I flew a lot together. It was early fall, and we were planning a trip next summer. We planned a round trip all over the United States. We were going to depart west on the southern route. We planned to stop at all the historical and geographical spots. To name a few: the Grand Canyon, Death Valley, Yosemite National Park, Washington, Oregon, Yellowstone National Park, and the Black Hills.

Around Thanksgiving time that year, my girlfriend Dolores (whom in the future I will refer to as Dee) and I were starting to get serious. We talked mildly of getting married.

On December 15, I remember the date very well; I went to the post office to get the mail. There was a very official-looking letter for me. I opened it, and I am sure you know what it said. It was from the president of the United States. I was drafted.

This sped things up a little. I was making pretty good payments on the loan. I decided that the airplane had to go I couldn't pay payments and hanger rent on army pay.

I called a man who bugged me to sell it to him many times. I asked him if he was still interested in buying the plane. He asked if I was selling it. I said if the price was right. He offered me a hundred dollars less than what I had paid for it. I sold it to him. I took the money and paid off my loan.

Several days later, I asked my mother to go shopping with me. We picked out a ring set for Dee. I gave it to her on Christmas eve. She was exited. I told her I was drafted, and we set the wedding date to be my first leave home.

2

I WAS INDUCTED INTO THE army on January 15, 1952. I went to Fort Mead, Maryland, for processing. I took all kinds of tests. I remember the one I took to see what I was best suited for; I scored one hundred in the mechanical section. They asked me what I wanted to do in the army. I told them I wanted to fly liaison pilot. He told me that I should apply after training. They told me I would be a wizz in the motor pool. After that, they stamped my papers for sixteen weeks of light weapons basic training. After getting issued my clothing which fit like a glove (if you know what I mean) and getting my shots, I was shipped out after being there for about five days.

On the third day, after evening chow, I got called on the bitch box to go to the orderly room. When I got there, they told me I had visitors at the service club. I wondered who in the hell would come and see me since I had only been gone for three days. I thought it might be a few of my friends who didn't have anything better to do. When I walked into the service dub, the first person I saw was Dolores's mother, and then I saw Dee. Mrs. Moore said, "We had to bring this girl down here. She's been crying ever since you left." Her mother, sister, and brother-in-law brought her down. They visited until late that evening.

I was sent to Camp Breckenridge Kentucky and assigned to the one hundred and first airborne for basic. Their basic training was the toughest there ever was, so I won't go into detail. I'll Just say that I went through sixteen weeks of hell. The last week of basic training, they took us in, one at a time and asked what we would like to do in the army. I again told them I wanted to fly. I told them I was a pilot and had my own plane. They explained to me that I had to be an officer to fly, and to be an officer, I would have to rejoin for three years right then and there and apply for officer candidate school. I decided against it. He then talked me into applying for the basic leadership course which I did.

When our orders came out, I was accepted for leadership school. It was an eight-week school on the same post. I got a five-day leave, but by the time, I got home there were only four days left. Dee and I decided to wait until my next leave to get married.

I went back to Breckenridge for eight weeks of leadership school. Upon completion of this school, they asked if anyone was interested in volunteering for airborne. I knew where I was going if I didn't. I thought it would be the only chance I would get to fly. Yet the thought of Jumping out of a perfectly good airplane didn't appeal to me, but I volunteered anyway.

I got a seven-day leave after leadership school ended. Again there was not enough time to get married because there was a three-day waiting period to get the licenses. We tried anyway. I wore my uniform to get the licenses and showed the clerk my orders. She sent me to see a Judge after looking at them. He waved the three day-waiting period, and we were married the next day August 17, 1952. We had a small wedding at Dee's church. The two immediate families were all that were there.

Three days later, I reported to Fort Benning, Georgia. I was there for about five weeks. During those weeks, I completed a three-week basic airborne course. The first week, we worked on PLF (parachute landing falls) and learned to exit the aircraft using the thirty-four foot towers. The second week, we used the two hundred and fifty foot towers. This was to teach us to guide the chute while descending. The third week, we made five parachute jumps. I left there as a qualified parachutist. My orders were for the far eastern command.

Let me describe jumping to you. For those of you who have never done it; jumping out of the airplane is the hardest. The mental block and the fear of height is there. You don't want to go, but you do. After leaving the plane, there is no sensation of falling. You leave an airplane that is doing 135 miles per hour. You are falling about 170 feet per second. The chute opens with a pop, and you almost stop instantly. The opening shock is indescribable. After the opening shock, the ride down is the most beautiful and peaceful thing that will ever happen to you. The stillness is unbelievable. There is no sensation of falling. You don't even know you are moving until you look down. The ground looks like it is gently floating up toward you.

After another leave home, I reported to the west coast where I was processed for shipping out. We flew out of there in a huge transport. I think it was a C-124. I remember looking back at the coast and wondering if I would ever see it again.

After several stops and a long tiresome flight, we arrived in Korea. Shortly after we arrived, a short truck ride took us to the replacement company. It was a short stop for the airborne men. We were no sooner there when they told us to get the bags and baggage out of the trucks. There were two trucks for us. We then went for a five-hour ride and stopped at a place that looked like a field hospital. We spent the night there. The men didn't talk too much, so we could scarcely hear the sounds of battle. I guess it was because they knew where they were going, and when we got there, we would get split up. I guess they had their minds on tomorrow. It was late October, and the night was cold,

Early the next morning after we had chow, we once again routed out and loaded on trucks. This time we got about a one-hour ride. The officer that we had met earlier that morning ordered us out. He explained that it was shorter and quicker to walk. We started cross country. After about a one-half-hour march, we came to the regimental headquarters of the 187 Airborne Regimental Combat Team.

After a pep talk by the executive officer, I was assigned to Easy Company Second Battalion. The sergeant from easy company took four of us. We walked for about a mile until we came to a hill top where the company was dug in. It wasn't a very big hill. It had a long gentle slope facing the direction of the enemy. It was a clear field for about three hundred yards and then woods. I looked it all over. There were no signs of battle, and everything was calm and peaceful.

I got assigned to the weapons platoon. I was ammo bearer for a fifty-seven recoilless rifle. I voiced my objections because I wanted a rifle. I didn't get a rifle but a mild chewing out for it.

It was mid-morning when I got to talking with my new buddies. I found out they had relieved another outfit that was there. They had been there for about ten days and were getting replacements every day. They told me they were way under strength when they came up here. This worried me. I thought I would get an outfit with a lot of seasoned vets in it. We still need one man to bring the squad up to full strength. We got him that afternoon.

He was a black man from Philadelphia. His name was Davis. The gunner's name was Jones, and he was also black. I forgot where he was from. He said he only had short time to rotate. I only knew him a few weeks before he was shipped out. The assistant gunner was a man of Spanish decent. I forgot his name. He was from Texas. He moved up to gunner on another gun in a few days. The other ammo bearer was a boy named Castle from Ohio. The only veterans in the squad were the gunner, assistant gunner, and the squad leader, whom I hadn't met yet.

The three new men fired questions at them most of the afternoon. I found out that things had been peaceful since they had been there. I also found why we didn't meet the platoon sergeant or the squad leader. They were having a meeting at the company command post. When they got back, we found out that the platoon sergeant was a big man named Rice who was from Ohio. Sergeant Pine from Texas was to be my squad leader. He was an average-sized man with sandy colored hair. He pulled the squad together and told us what went on at the platoon meeting.

They were told the enemy had pulled out of this section. The next morning, we were sending out a patrol to see if this was so. If it was, they were to continue until they made contact.

The next morning after chow, the patrol was to go out. I felt sorry for them but glad it was them and not me. But that was not to be. One of the men who was to go out cut himself in the thigh with entrenching knife. The first sergeant started yelling, "I need another man. All right, where is the guy who wants to be a rifle man, now get over there and get briefed?" He came right over to me and said, "Get yourself a rifle and ammo. Your squad leader will lend you his."

I got two bandoliers for the MI and two grenades. I then doubled time to the sergeant in charge of the patrol. He looked at the grenades hanging on my ammo belt along with the two bandoliers and said, "What the hell are you going to do? Lick them by yourself,"

He explained to me what they were going to do very quickly. We were going to move across the open field in a skirmisher and close it up into a diamond. We reached the woods, and he said, "You'll be alright if you keep an eye on me."

We went across the field. My knees were shaking, and sweat was running down my face even though it was quite cold that morning. It was a clear sunny morning. The wind was calm, and everything seemed very quiet. I could even hear my heart beat. We got to the woods and closed in on the sergeant. Everyone moved into a diamond. I got the left flank. I thought that the sergeant would change that. I didn't think he would want a green man out there, but he looked over the formation and motioned to go on. I didn't like my position. But I had to make the best of it and kept my dam eyes and ears open.

We were still moving down the slope through the woods. We must have gone a hundred yards or more when I thought we were going to be all right. My nerves were just starting to calm down when it happened. A machine gun started to fire. It sounded like it was about a hundred yards ahead of me and off to my right. I fell right to my face and rolled over and looked for the sergeant. I could see the rest of the patrol running and jumping for cover. I also saw the bark and the dead tree limbs being knocked off the trees around them. They seemed to be firing high. I noticed none of the firing was coming near me. I got up on one knee and tried to see the gun, but I couldn't see it. I knew that this meant they couldn't see me. I sat there for a few moments wondering what the hell to do. I looked at the sergeant, but I saw he was busy. It looked like they lowered their fire, and it was coming several feet off the ground. Everyone over there was crawling on their stomach getting behind a tree, log, or stump.

All the sudden, a thought scared me half to death. I quickly looked off to my left wondering if we were going to be flanked by the enemy infantry. I saw a few yards away a dry wash. The kind that only runs for a few days after a rain. It was only a few feet deep. It was going down the slope and getting deeper as it went. I got up and ran and dove into it. I lay there a minute to see if I had drawn fire; I hadn't. I sat in the wash and wondered again, "What the hell was I to do now?" I thought I could maybe move down it and flank that gun. I crawled down the wash for thirty or forty yards. It was then deep enough to run in a crouch. I got up and had run for a few more yards when I came to a turn in it. It turned toward the gun. I hugged the right bank and decided what to do. It sounded like the enemy gun was still way ahead of me and off to the right. Then a sickening thought entered my mind. I thought they would surely have had this wash covered with a rifle. I got my MI ready and charged around the turn in the wash. Once again, I threw myself on the left bank. I lay there against the bank and strained my eyes to see if they had covered this wash. I saw nothing.

The gun stopped, and everything got quiet. I told myself to stay put because if I had moved, they would have surely heard me.

The gun started again. I ran further down the wash and kept bearing to my right toward the gun. I kept running until I thought that I was right off its flank. I hugged the right bank next to the gun. It was blasting away while I crawled up the bank. I peered over it, and there it was. I was only a few yards past it. There were five of them. I could see two on the gun, one kneeling down behind it and one man on each flank only five or ten yards from the gun.

They were busy looking ahead of them. The gun was only about thirty yards away. I crouched back down out of sight of them. I thought about what to do again. I gripped my MI. I thought I could rise up firing and get the gunner and the assistant, hopefully before they could return the fire. I also thought when they returned it, there would be three of them firing at me and pin me down in the wash. Then it would only have been a matter of time until I bought it.

My hand instantly went down to my ammo belt, and I picked off one of the grenades. I thought this would be much better. They wouldn't know where it came from. The ones the grenade didn't get, I would have a better chance with.

I pulled the pin and raised it up while they were looking straight ahead. I released the lever and threw it immediately. Its range was beautiful. It landed about eight to ten feet behind the man crouched behind the gun. I dove back down waiting on the report of the grenade. When it finally blew, I could feel the earth beneath me tremble. I got my MI ready and raised it up sharply ready to fire. It wasn't necessary, for the grenade had done its job. The man that was kneeling behind the gun was now eight to ten feet out in front of it lying face down. The other two men that were manning the gun were lying slightly forward of their position. The gun was lying on its side, and the man nearest to me was just about in the same place. He was lying face up. The man on the far flank was laying on his side. His back was toward me, and he was moving slightly with a low moan.

I went back down and came up slowly looking all around. I strained my eyes looking back through the woods for more. I could see no one, so I rose up on one knee bracing myself with my MI and looked again at what I had done.

The first thought that went through my mind was, "What gave me the right to do this?" I was holding back the vomit when the next thoughts I had were very strange. I wondered how many people would weep or grieve over what I had done. I also wondered if the Chinese army notified their next of kin, I was about ready to cry.

The company must have moved up in support when the firing had started. One of the first few men to get to me was the sergeant. He grabbed my hand and shook it. He said, "I'll be damned. After all the replacements I had, I finally got a killer." I looked up at him. The look on my face must have done it. The smile went off his face, and he walked away. He had ordered the medic to check over them.

A Lieutenant Williams, who was later to become my platoon leader walked over to me. He asked if I was all right; I told him that I was sick, and that I was not a killer. He knew that I was not proud of what I had done.

He grasped my shoulder and gave a gentle tug on it. Then he said, "You'll be all right, son. If you were acting like a barnyard rooster and bragging about it, then I would worry about you."

Just then the medic yelled at the first sergeant, "They're all dead."

I jumped up and said, "No, the far one is still alive."

The lieutenant asked the medic to check again. He checked again and said, "The man is dead, sir," I hung my head. The lieutenant patted me on the back.

I sat there thinking, "My, god. It's only my second day here, and I've already killed five men."

The lieutenant came back to me and said, "When the patrol goes on, you go with it. If you don't, your next one will really be tough." He told me that they might try to replace me and insisted that I should go. He told me that it was the best thing that I could do.

They formed up the patrol. I guess I didn't look very good because the sergeant in charge of the patrol came over to me and softly asked if I wanted to be replaced. You couldn't know how bad I did, but I thought about what the lieutenant had said and shook my head no.

The patrol went on down the gentle slope for a distance and then came to a small creek. We crossed it and started uphill. I couldn't get what had happened out of my mind. I could still hear that gun blasting away. I thought about how loud it was. It hit me that the enemy must have heard it, too, and that they would know we were coming. I hoped that they had withdrawn, hoping that the gun was still there.

We were about halfway up the hill when the possibility of them being on top hit me. If we were to catch hell, it would be any time now. Again the sweat rolled down my face. We kept going, and we were not far from the top. I kept thinking to myself, "What were they waiting for?" We made it to the top of the hill. They weren't there. The sergeant singled to hold up. He sent two men out. One man went to the right and one to the left. He told them to go a couple hundred yards to have a look. While we sat there, most of the men lit a cigarette. I didn't smoke. I think every man including the sergeant offered me one. I refused them, explaining that I didn't smoke. Several of the men asked for a light, but I had none.

The men came back and said they had seen nothing. The sergeant looked across the valley at the next hill. He said, "They must be over there." He formed us up, and we moved out. We moved down the hill and toward the valley and the other hill. We crossed the narrow valley and started up the other hill. We had only gone several hundred yards and were not quite up yet when someone yelled, "Hit the dirt!" There was a small tree just ahead of me. I dove behind it, and the shooting started.

I looked out around the tree. I could see them. They were a few trees and some rocks aways up the hill. We started to return the fire. I brought my MI up and started firing rapidly into the trees. I looked over at the sergeant. He was on his radio. I just kept on firing. The next thing I knew, the sergeant was waving and yelling to get the hell out of there. We stopped firing and ran back down the hill. After we had run about a hundred yards, they stopped firing. We had no casualties. We went back up to the top of the first hill we were on. When we got there, the sergeant stopped us and told one man to go back down the hill a distance and keep his eyes open. He then told the rest of the patrol to take a breather. He said that the company was coming up. When they arrived, I saw the patrol leader explaining where we made contact with the enemy.

Each platoon was given a section. We were told to dig because we would be here for a while. My squad was the first squad of the fifty-seven section weapons platoon, and we were assigned to the first platoon. We were there for a longtime with just patrolling action. I had had my share of that, for patrolling had little action.

Rumors had it that we were going to be there for the winter. I believed it was too late to start anything. By the looks of the sky and our daily temperature, I thought we would get our first snow any day.

Advancement and rank came fast. The men were rotating and shifting around to take their places. By late November, I was assistant gunner. I wasn't there for two weeks when I moved up to gunner in Mid-December.

It was about this time that I got word. I was wanted at the company command post. To get there I had to pass the mess tent. As I walked past it, I caught view of the executive officer. He called to me as I passed. He wanted to talk to me. I asked if I could speak to him on the way back because I was wanted at the command post. He told me that he was the one who sent for me. He offered me a cup of coffee and asked me to sit down with him.

As soon as I got seated, he asked how my wife was. He asked how my parents, brothers, sisters, and close relatives were.

I paused and just stared at him. He was beginning to worry me. I was starting to think that something was wrong back home. I answered, "The last time I heard from them, they were fine, sir."

He said, "You do want to hear from them don't you?" He continued, "Then why in the hell don't they hear from you? Why do they have to inquire through the Red Cross about your well-being?"

I just looked down at the table. After a few moments passed, I said, "I guess I have been neglecting them, sir."

He said, "Can you imagine how they feel about you being over here in a combat zone and not hearing from you?"

I told him that I would take care of it.

He said, "Do it right now." He reached behind him and got some writing paper and envelopes. He put them in front of me along with a pen. He said that there was plenty of coffee there. I want you to write everyone you know on a regular basis.

I said, "It won't happen again, sir." He just smiled and walked out.

I wrote to my mother and father and then to Dee. I apologized to them for not writing sooner. I promised to write more often in the future. I never mentioned to them what had happened. I made myself a promise that in the future to write at least once a week, even if just to say hello, and that I was fine and hoped that they were the same.

I finished the letters and took them to the company command post. I gave them to the company clerk to mail. The executive officer was there. I looked over at him as I was getting ready to leave when he gave a slight nod of his head and winked at me.

As I left the command post, I thought they should get the letters for Christmas or a few days before. I then realized that I never even said anything about Christmas. I thought that I would write another tomorrow.

The next day, when I was just getting ready to write a couple of letters, the USO brought Christmas cards around to us. As they passed them out, they said that they would see to it that our families would get them for Christmas. I wrote a few lines in each one of them that I sent.

From that time on, I wrote as often as I could, usually two or three times a week. Dee wrote every day. Her letters came like clockwork. I really looked forward to them.

Christmas was fast approaching. The army did all they could do to make it seem like Christmas. We got our hot traditional Christmas dinner. They set up a few speakers. They played Christmas carols. They played the faster peppy ones like "Jingle Bells," "Here Comes Santa Clause," and "the Twelve days of Christmas."

The ones the army neglected to play, the enemy took good care of. They set up speakers and played Christmas carols too. They were quite fond of "I'll be Home for Christmas," "I'll have a Blue Christmas without You," "Silver Bells," "Silent Night," and "I'm Dreaming of a White Christmas."

Several times, an officer would come around and tell us to buckle down and not to let it get to us. He said that they were using psychological warfare. I didn't care what they called it. They were hitting us close to home.

In early January, the section sergeant rotated us. Usually when a man rotated, he gave away his personal property and things that were hard to get. Expensive things some men offered to buy. I offered to buy the sergeants cigarette lighter. Several others did the same. He asked me why I wanted it when I didn't smoke. I explained that I was always being asked for a light, and that if I had it, it would be like community property. He gave it to me with some spare flints and fluid.

I thought that now I would be ready for them. I wouldn't have to carry matches anymore. They usually got wet from rain or body perspiration. I thought that as much as it would be used, the flint and fluid would last a long time.

My squad leader got his job, and I wondered who we would get next for a squad leader. The next day, Sergeant Chestnut sent for me, and I went back to his tent. He said there were men with more time in grade in the section that he had approached for the job of squad leader. He said that they had all turned it down for one reason or another. He asked me if I wanted it. He said, "I think you can handle it all right." He told me he wanted me to take it. I thought about it for a few minutes and then accepted. The rank of sergeant went with it and an MI rifle. On the way back to the squad, I realized what the hell I had done. I would not go on patrols anymore. I would take the patrols out and make the decisions that might get men killed. The whole thought scared me.

Through the cold winter months, there wasn't much action. We would go over and spy on the enemy, making sure that they were not up to anything. They did the same to us. There was very little action involving the patrols. They went out on a daily basis. I'm sure the enemy patrol also did the same.

I was just getting used to them as the weather warmed up, and the snow disappeared. Shortly after the snow was all gone, the company runner went to the sergeant's tent. He was there a short time and left. Sergeant Chestnut came out and called me, and I went over to him. He said, "The old man wants to see you."

I thought to myself, "What the hell does he want?"

I went to the company commander. He was a tall man in his late twenties. That is all I will say about him. My philosophy was if you can't say anything nice about a person, don't say anything at all. He told me to sit down. He said that we had been cooling our heels long enough. He wanted me to take over a patrol and raise some hell. He looked at me and said, "Do you think you can do that?"

I replied, "Yes, sir." I began to work out the details with the first sergeant and the section sergeant.

I went to the first sergeant. When I got there, my section sergeant was already there. They both looked at me like I should be mad or griping. I just said, "How the hell are we going to do this?" They explained that the old man was getting restless and bucking for rank.

We sat down and agreed the patrol would consist of seven men and myself. Sergeant Chestnut asked who I wanted. I told him Davis and Castel for sure. He named some men from another squad and gave me my ammo bearers. I explained that they had been here for only a short time and should be getting their feet wet. Two of them were from the state of Washington. They looked like brothers but were not related. The other man was from Indiana. We all agreed that it was getting late, and that we would be going out at eight-thirty hours the next morning.

I went back and rounded up the men to go. I told them what we had to do. I had no specific plans of what we were really going to do though. He decided we would play it by ear when we got there. I said, "Once we're there, we'll see what happens and ask for suggestions." They all agreed on my plan.

The next morning, we armed ourselves to the teeth and moved out. We went past our outpost, who knew where we were going and for what reason. Everyone in the company knew by now. They all wished us good luck and good hunting. I gave them a half-smile and said, "Thanks." Our job was to go over and raise some hell and kill a few of them. The thought didn't appeal to me or anybody else that was going.

We moved to the valley down below and stopped. I didn't want the enemy to know where we were until we started raising hell. I told them to avoid any on the way.

I put Castel on the point and told him to stay about a hundred yards ahead. I gave him specific orders that if he saw anything to get his tail back here immediately. I told Davis to drop back a safe distance to cover our rear. We started up a trail through some woods, and I thought that we must be getting close to their lines.

When Castel came back, he told me that he could see them from the next raise and pointed to it. I asked him how far away they were. He replied, "About one hundred and fifty yards out." There was a lot of activity over there so he assumed that something was up. I got my field glasses out and was going to move up with him. Just as I was about to start, Davis came double time in and told us that there was an enemy patrol coming right up behind us. We were in the middle and had to do something fast. I told Davis to go back as far as he could and let them go by. I said, "Watch to see if they have a rear guard." I told the rest of the patrol to get off the trail and out of sight. I spread them out from forty to fifty yards off the trail. I told them not to fire unless they see us or if I fire.

We were not much more than out of sight when we heard them coming. They were laughing and carrying on as if they had just seen something comical. They had passed my first man and were coming along the trail toward me. I was in some brush and didn't know if they saw me or not. All eleven of them continued to laugh. When they were almost directly in front of me, the one in the lead looked right toward me. I thought that if he saw me, he may walk right by me and then come back. I slowly raised my MI. and got him in sight. I could see him smiling. Sweat rolled down my face. My heart pounded. I never had one in my sights before, and I knew that if I pulled the trigger that he would be no more. I thought, "If he was in my position that I would be a dead man." I pulled the trigger. The report of the rifle was loud, and the recoil jarred my body. He went down like a ton of bricks had fallen on him. At the same instant, the rest of the patrol opened up. It only lasted about five seconds. We all ran over to them. I told Castel to get on the raise and keep his eyes open. I told the two men from Washington to search them quickly. Moments later, Davis came in and said the back door was clear. I motioned for Castel to come back. The two men gave me some papers they had found on the bodies. I put them inside my field jacket. I told them we are going home.

Davis objected and said that the old man wasn't going to like it. "'We never made it through their lines, and if I know him, he'll send us back over to get the job done."

I quickly spoke up. "If this patrol would go on, we'd never make it. They know we're here, and they're going to be ready for us. They may be half way here by now, so let's get the hell out of here."

I told Davis to take the point and move at a fast pace. Castel was to take the rear and watch behind us. This way we could move at a quicker pace.

No one talked much going home, and I had time to think about what we had done. They never had a chance. We just slaughtered them. They never knew what hit them.

When I got back, I reported to the company commander and told him what had happened. I gave him my papers. We took off the dead enemy. I told him that the enemy suffered eleven dead. We had no casualties. He asked if I had reached their lines. I said, "No, sir. We got approximately one hundred fifty yards from them when this action occurred." He started to chew me out. I interrupted him by saying, "Sir, for this patrol to go on would be suicide. They knew we were there, and just about where we were, we fired very close to their lines. To continue on, we would of had the same fate as their patrol." The executive officer was sitting there and said in a low voice, "I agree." The company commander dismissed me.

As I walked out of the command post, I heard the company commander yelling at the executive officer, "When I am reprimanding one of my men, you stay the hell out of it."

The executive officer said, "Reprimand hell. You should have hung a metal on him." A half smile came across my face as I walked back to the squad. When I got back, they all wanted to know what happened. I told them to relax; everything was okay.

After getting back and seated in our position, I had time to think about what we had done and how we had done it. Sergeant Chestnut came over and said, "I heard what you did. How was it?" I told him that I was feeling kind of squeamish and told him that we had slaughtered them. He said as he walked away, "Hell, that's what we're here for. Don't let that bother you."

About two hours later, Lieutenant Williams came over to me with another officer. He introduced me and told him that I was the officer in charge of the patrol. He asked me where I found them and what time. I told him what he wanted to know. He told me I ought to be damn glad that I did it. The two officers looked at one another. The one that I was just introduced to said, "Hell, you're going to find out anyway. They found the bodies of two GIs in the Charlie company sector that were so mutilated that their own mothers wouldn't have recognized them. He told me that it was done early that morning. "They had to be the ones that did it." I told him how they were laughting and carrying on about something that was funny to them.

He kicked his foot into the ground and said, "I am glad you got them. I'm damn glad you got them. I would hate for them to think that they got away with something like this. I hope that they think we chased them all the way there to get them." Both Lieutenant Williams and the other officer walked away.

Several days later, we were ordered to take that same hill. After an artillery pounding, we took it without firing a shot. The enemy withdrew to the next hill. About a half mile away, we saw what looked like a swamp. We dug in wondering why the enemy gave us the hill. I asked Lieutenant Williams about it. He said that they were out in front of their lines. In other words, they had their necks stretched out. He said, "They will probably give us the one over there too. But I still think that they are in front of that one."

We were there for a few days. We could hear heavy firing to our east. We assumed someone was catching hell, but we had no idea who.

It was mid-morning when word came down that there was a platoon leaders and platoon sergeant meeting at the company command post. Everyone that had been there for any length of time knew that this meant bad news. They came back an hour before noon chow and called a squad leader meeting at the platoon command post. The other squad leaders and I went over to the command post; We were told the bad news.

A leg outfit was trying to take over hill number 38 without success. (A leg outfit is one that is not airborne. I don't know where they got this name. There is no disrespect meant by this name. I think it comes from ours and their class A uniforms. We wore blouse boots. They wore low quarter shoes. The name came from straight leg and "leg" for short. It was the airborne way of distinguishing one from the other. They probably called us bone heads. I don't know.) It was going to be our job to drop eleven miles behind that hill at night and move up to the base of the rear. We were to wait until the artillery was lifted and stick them, hopefully by surprise.

George and Fox company units were to hold our position until we got back. The platoon leader and sergeant called two squads at a time from the platoon. We were briefed over and over again which took all afternoon. We were to jump eleven miles behind their lines and move up to the reverse side of the hill and wait for the artillery barrage to lift. The leg outfit would fake a frontal attack while we went up the rear of the hill and over the top catching them by surprise.

Early the next morning, units of George and Fox companies moved into our positions. We pulled back for several miles. We were met by trucks. We rode the rest of the night and almost all the next day. Late that afternoon, we met our destination, an airfield.

There were quite a few propeller type fighters and a few small two engine bombers. There were four C119's parked at the one end. We rode up to where they were and were issued chutes and stick orders. I was in the middle of the right stick. The whole company was briefed again, and we got one meal of C rations, our ammo, and a hot meal.

We then laid around under the planes waiting for time to go. The men smoked a lot. I think they used my lighter a dozen times. I got kidded about having it. Several tried to buy it, but I still wouldn't sell it.

It was starting to get dusk when a truck pulled up with the air force crews. We then loaded up and sat there for at least a half hour before they started the engines. Then we waited another twenty minutes before we started to move. We were soon airborne and on our way, about an hour after, dark. We rode for about one hour and fifteen minutes changing directions several times. I knew this and wondered how many of the men knew when we changed courses. We then got the fifteen-minute warning. The officer went up and down the aisles yelling, "Don't forget your assembly area. Go southwest when you get down. It will be dark, and you will be in strange territory, but if you move southwest, you should be all right." I kept watching the two lights. One was red and one green. The red one came on when there was five minutes to go. When it came on, the lieutenant moved to the doors which were already open. He yelled, "Both sticks get ready." He paused for a second and said, "Stand up, hook up, and check your equipment." After a short time, came sound off with equipment check. It came twenty okay, nineteen okay, eighteen okay and so on down the line. We were then supposed to shuffle and stand in the door. We waited for the green light. When it came on, he yelled, "Go!" We started to go. The average time for twenty men to get out of one door is seven or eight seconds.

Before I knew it, I was checking my canopy. The ride down seemed short. I landed, and it seemed like quite a few men around me. Two men from each squad were assigned to dig holes to bury the chutes in. I saw a hole being dug, so I threw my chute beside it and told them to put it in when they were finished. I then moved southwest, and soon I came to the assembly area. I checked in with the first sergeant to see how many of my men checked in and to find out where he wanted my squad. He told me, and I went over to the area he specified. Two of the squad were already there, and soon they were all in. I gave a sigh of relief.

We were there for an hour or more, and I thought we should be moving. I went over to the command post where I found most of the officers and non-commission officers. I asked what the hell was going on. I was told that we are not where we were supposed to be, and none of the land marks checked with our maps.

The company executive officer who was in charge sent four patrols out in all directions. They were to find land marks such as roads, railroads, bridges, crossroads, or high ridges. He told them not to be gone for more than one hour. They came back with all kinds of landmarks. The one that went west found a road that crossed a large creek. Then shortly after that, it came to a crossroad. The man that went east found a large creek with an old railroad bridge over it. The one going north said there was a small town or village in the next valley, and the man going south found a large creek. We thought it was the same one the patrol going west found.

The officer and platoon sergeant started checking their maps. They were checking for several minutes when Lieutenant Williams said, "Holly hell look here!" The officers crowded around him. He pointed out what he found, and they all looked at their own maps. After a short time, they agreed that he was right. One of the men said, "Boy, are we in trouble." The platoon sergeants were already there. The area where we were was marked on their maps. Then they went back to their platoons.

I walked back with Sergeant Rice. He was mumbling and cursing to himself, so I didn't say anything on the way over to the platoon. He passed the word for a squad leader meeting. That's where we got the news. He said as far as they could tell we were eighty-one miles too far behind the lines and in big trouble; we were also too far for help of any kind.

The executive officer passed word for another platoon sergeant meeting. He had a patrol watching the road to our west, and he explained what he was going to do. "If we are where I think we are, that road goes damn near right to our objective." He said he was calling in the patrol. If they had seen nothing, we were going right down that road in a force march.

He called in the patrol, and they had seen nothing. So out to and onto the road we went. It was about 0100 hours when we hit the road. All through the night, we walked the road without incident. Dawn was starting to break, and we all came to a patch of woods several hundred yards from the road. The executive officer called a halt. We took cover on the sides of the road and sent the patrol over to the woods to check them out. Several minutes after going into the woods, they came out and waved at us to come on. We moved into the woods where we were told to put out security and then take a rest.

They had someone watching the road. We stayed there several hours. Then the executive officer called in the patrol and asked what they had seen. They said they had seen nothing. He wanted to move out. He said, "I would hate like hell to get caught out here." He and his officers pondered the situation for a while. Then he said, "What the hell? We're going. If we get caught, at least it will be closer to home." Off and on was the order, and we again moved down the road in force march. It was about 1000 hours when we started again.

3

WE WENT THROUGH THE MORNING and into the afternoon without incidents. We had seen some civilians who waved and smiled at us. I don't think they even knew what side we were on.

On several occasions, we saw a squadron of jet fighters flying parallel to us over the horizon. Late into the afternoon, we saw a squadron of them off to our right. They were flying parallel to us only about a mile away. I saw the executive officer getting out a flare gun. He was frantically going through some flares looking for the right colors when the plane in the lead did a victory roll.

Nobody said anything. I looked around and saw quite a few smiling faces. I think everyone's heart was beating a little easier now. We were not alone. They knew we were there. We at least owned the sky.

We had one meal of C rations with us. I saw some of the men eating as we marched. I got the man behind me to get mine out of my backpack. I had some beans and franks. I opened them and ate them while force marching down the road. They were quite cold, but everything was nourishing.

We marched on into the evening without incidents. Shortly after dark, I could hear some of the men beginning to gripe. We came to a crossroad, and one officer wanted to hold up and check the maps. The executive officer said, "I already have, and we go straight ahead."

The lead didn't much more than get through the crossroad when a machine gun started. They were firing over our heads. They stopped and said something in Chinese. I got quiet then for a few seconds. We were all hugging the ground. They fired a few more bursts over our heads when our interpretator started to yell back to them in Chinese. They said something back, and he answered them. He then got up and motioned for the rest to do so.

We got up and continued on down the road. I later asked him what he had said. He said to translate it was something like this. "What the hell's the matter with you knuckle heads firing at troops this far behind lines. They said that they heard somebody speaking English. I said, you're damn right we have English speaking troops in this outfit. Now we are going to pass. Then he said, hell I didn't even lie to them did I."

We continued on through the night without incident and without much English being spoken. About 0300 hours, the executive officer called another halt. We were alongside of some woods. He had them checked out, and they were clean. We moved in about a hundred yards off the road. We were told again to put out security and rest. He called a platoon leaders and sergeants meeting. We thought that we must be getting close. We could hear some firing off in the distance. The platoon leaders and sergeants came back in half an hour.

Then they called a squad leaders meeting. They briefed us on what was going on. The executive officer said he thought we were close to the objective. He thought we were less than a mile away. He told us that we would stay here until daylight which was about an hour away. We would then move out to the back side of the hill. They decided not to break radio silence to ask for artillery. The executive officer thought we could get them by total surprise right after morning chow. If there was no firing, they would be relaxing.

The time came, and we moved out. We went to what we thought was the backside of the hill. The word was passed. "Make damn sure the enemy is up there before we start to fire." Our troops might have taken it. We crept up the hill. Just before going over the top, we formed a skirmisher. Then the order came over the top. The fifty-seven squads followed a few yards behind the infantry. As I topped the hill, I thought our men were cracking up. I saw some of them firing in the air and laughing. A few more yards, and I saw what was going on.

We literally caught them with their pants down. I saw some bare buttocks going down over the hill. Some of them were carrying their steel pots like they had something in them that they didn't want to spill. Very few had weapons. I saw one bare buttock going down through some trees. He was dragging his rifle. He stopped and I thought he was going to pick up his rifle. I fired four or five rounds well over his head. He dropped everything and started to run again. I looked around, and everyone was about to split a gut laughing. The really funny part about it was that they were running away from us and right into the leg outfit's waiting arms. This was the lift Easy company really needed. They went through one hell of a lot in the last twenty-four hours. I thought that they were nearing the end of their endurance.

I looked around, and there were stacks of rifles scattered here and there. They must have thought they weren't going to need them to stack them. There were machine guns with belts of ammo in them. They were ready to go and had never fired a shot. I saw one mortar down. It looked like it was being cleaned.

We made a gift of the hill. We gave it to the company commander of the leg outfit. He was a captain. I saw him and our commander talking. I moved over the hill to hear what they were saying. Our executive officer said, "Here is your hill. Sorry, we are a day late." It was through no fault of ours. He then asked if the captain could spare a meal for his troops. The captain refused and said that it would cut his men short. The executive officer said, "Hell, these men just forced marched over eighty miles in twenty-four hours on one meal of C rations." The captain still refused. He then asked for transportation back to our position. He refused again and said that there were no trucks available. The executive officer called him ungrateful and a few more unpleasant names.

He came back to the men who were all griping. He gathered the men and explained in a loud voice so that the leg captain could hear. He said, "We are going to rest here before going home if our host doesn't mind. Our good host will not feed us nor furnish transportation home, so it looks like we are going to have to walk home on an empty stomach."

We rested there until about 1400 hours. After about two hours back on the road, the executive officer contacted the company command post. He told them where we were and ordered the mess sergeant to get a hot meal ready. He was to meet us on the road. We continued for about three hours. It was getting dark when he called a halt. He said, "We will wait here for chow." I don't think I could have gotten back up to go on if I had to.

The mess truck got there about ten minutes later. They sat up the chow line. We started through it. They had beef stew, bread, and hot coffee. It started to rain as I was being served. I went over to a log and sat on it to eat. The rain was running off my steel pot. It looked like muddy water and was running into my stew. I thought it would be all right because it would blend right in with the gravy. The bread was stale, and it snapped like a cracker. I ate it and thought it was good. I hate black coffee, but that coffee was delicious. I still think of that as the best meal I've ever eaten.

After the meal, I looked around. Most of the men were sleeping with the rain hitting them right in the face. It stopped raining a short time later. The executive officer said that the men can't go on. We were to spend the night there. He called the company command post and told them what he was planning to do. He got the okay.

That was the worst night that I have ever spent. The moon came out, and the temperature started to drop. The only thing we had beside what we were wearing was a poncho. I was wet and rolled up in my poncho. I soon found out that was no good. My breath was condensing and sweating up my poncho and was getting me wetter. I put my head out from under it. I soon had to cover it again. It was really getting cold. I awoke in the morning shivering. My poncho was frozen with frost. We formed up and went home.

After arriving home, we settled back in our old positions. Everyone was well beat. The order came down and put out the outpost. We were to change them every two hours and rest. I think about ninety percent of the men were sleeping most of the day.

The next day about mid-morning, a full-bird colonel arrived. He was a leg. Most of the non-commission officers moved over to the company command post to see what the hell was going on.

He got the old man and started to chew him out. When the old man asked what for he was told that charges were being drawn up on the unit commander in charge of Easy Company for his actions on hill three hundred and eighty-four. The captain explained that it was not him. He told him that the executive officer was in charge of that hill. He sent for the executive officer.

When he arrived, he was told what was going on. He asked who was preparing the charges. He was told the name of the captain we gave the hill to. The executive officer told the colonel what had happened. He explained everything we had gone through and how we had taken the hill on one meal of C rations. He told him what the no good son of a bitch had refused to feed us or even give us some C rations. He also told him that he had refused to furnish transportation back here. He then called him an ungrateful son of a bitch and a few other choice names. He told him that he was the one who should be charged.

The colonel asked if he called his superiors before refusing.

The executive officer answered, no.

The colonel stood in silence for a few minutes and then said, "If you don't bring charges, I will see that the captain will be well reprimanded."

The executive officer said, "As far as I'm concerned, the whole matter is forgotten." They agreed, and the colonel apologized for his captain. The colonel left, and that was all that we heard of that.

Things were quiet and peaceful for several days. I would look down from the hill at the restful waters of the swamps. They were between us and the enemy. I would daydream of my home, wife, and family, wondering how everybody was. I would guess what they were doing. I tried not to think of those things. I thought that it would only make things worse. But the restful waters of the swamp seemed to hypnotize me.

We could see the enemy moving about on his hill. It was about four hundred yards across from us. I was sure he could see us too. We both went about our business as usual not paying any attention to one another.

I woke up one morning, and it was raining on and off and very cold. They called one of those meetings of platoon leaders and sergeants. They came back and held a squad leader meeting. We were ordered to take that hill. We were to send a patrol out that night to estimate the enemy strength and try to pinpoint his crew weapons (machine guns, mortars, and etc.). The information they came back with would determine the amount of artillery preparation we would get. We were to jump off at 7:10 the next, morning.

That evening, I was setting to eat my chow. When Davis came from getting his, he said, "Beaver the old man wants to see you." I swallowed my chow whole like a hog and started to the company command post wondering what the hell he wanted now. I didn't know it then, but the next twenty-four hours of my life proved that I had never walked alone.

I got to the command post, and the old man and a sergeant were there. Sergeant Altman was a tall thin man younger than I was, and he had been in the army longer. He was RA (regular army) which meant that he had enlisted. He was from somewhere in Eastern Pennsylvania. I knew the sergeant, but we weren't what you would call good buddies. I had nothing against him. It was just that we didn't see that much of one another to get to be buddies. It seemed that I would be on one end of the company sector, while he was on the other. He seemed all right to me as far as I knew him. I had never heard anything bad about him.

The old man explained that the sergeant was taking out the reconnaissance patrol that night. A reconnaissance patrol is one that goes out looking for information only. They avoid the enemy at all cost. He explained that he had mostly green men and asked if I would go with him.

I asked, "Why me?" I would think the sergeant would ask for someone he had worked with.

The old man answered for the sergeant. He said, "Sergeant Altman thinks you are a damn good man on patrol." He then added, "This is strictly voluntary, understand." The old man had his way of getting volunteers. He asked me in front of Sergeant Altman on purpose. I looked down at Sergeant Altman. His eyes were almost pleading. How are you to say no in front of a man begging you? I agreed to go. We went from there straight to a briefing with the company executive officer at the mess tent.

The other man was going to be there. All the way over there, Sergeant Altman thanked me for going. He seemed very sincere about it as if he really appreciated it.

At the briefing, we agreed to go over on the enemies far west flank and then work east along his lines. At the far east flank, the hill dropped into a valley with a road in it. We couldn't see the road from our position. When the hill started to drop off, we were to return across the swamp. The patrol consisted of five men. Sergeant Altman, three of his men, and me. We were to go out at twenty-one hundred hours.

I went back to the squad and told them what I was going to do. They all told me that I was crazy. I got ready to go. I took only six clips of ammo since this was a reconnaissance patrol. I checked my MI good to make sure it was working properly. I then had several hours to kill, so I tried to get some sleep. The next thing I knew, Davis was shaking me and saying it was time to go.

I reported to the third platoon and Sergeant Altman. He and his men were waiting for me. We reported to the company executive officer and set up a sign and a counter sign. He was to set it up with the outpost. We were to come back to our outpost between twenty-four hours and zero one hundred hours.

We moved to our far right flank and started down the hill. The three men were gabbing. I told them to knock it off. They would, and then they would start again. I told them several times. We came to the bottom of the hill and started across. It wasn't long before we were sinking into ankle deep mud. Then the water went to our knees, and the next thing we knew, we were waist deep in water. The green men must have thought it was funny. They were yelling and laughing. I thought it was damn cold. I turned to Sergeant Altman and asked him. "What the hell do these guys think this is, an overnight boy scout hike. You shut them up, or I will." They must have heard me because they shut up immediately. But it was too late. We started to get small arms fire from the base of the hill.

The green men started to scream and run back with Sergeant Altman after them hollering to get back here. I charged straight ahead as fast as I could in the water. They kept firing periodically. I knew the closer I got to the firing, the higher it would be over my head. At times, I was in water up to my armpits. I kept going until I had reached the far bank. I lay there to catch my breath. Then I heard some of them coming and firing out across the swamp. They would fire and then laugh. They must have been laughing at the green men screaming.

There was a small tree ahead of me with branches almost all the way to the ground. It reminded me of a Christmas tree, but it wasn't an evergreen. I hurriedly crawled over to it. I could hear them getting closer. I crawled under the tree. It was about four feet in diameter at the base. I wrapped myself around the trunk like a snake.

They came right down almost to me. One fired out across the water. Another one walked over within several feet of the tree. I held my breath. One of the other said something, and they all started to walk toward the hill. I lay there as they walked away. They were gabbing as they walked. I thought this was a golden opportunity to follow them right up the hill. I thought the noise they made along with their gabbing would cover up the noise I would make.

I crawled out from under the tree and slung my MI over my back and took a quick look around. I took off after them. I closed up on them until I could hear them pretty well. I followed them almost all the way to the top where they got challenged. It came from off to my left. The four men started to chew then out for the challenge. It sounded like they said, "You know damn well who is coming. What the hell is the matter with you?"

While this was going on, I moved several yards to my right and lay there for what seemed like half an hour. I could hear them talking. They must have been on their lines. It sounded like thirty yards up from me and off to my left. It was quiet off to my right, and I decided to crawl that way.

I crawled inch by inch feeling my way, so I wouldn't make any noise. I most have gone about halfway to the top. I could still hear them talking. I was bearing fairly hard to my right. I must have taken me a half an hour to go that far. Then I made a noise. They stopped talking suddenly. They all must have heard it. I lay there motionless listening to them. A short time later, they started to talk again. I lay there for a while listening to them and then started to crawl again. I only went several yards.

I saw several groups of two waiting around. Some were going from the tree lines back across the clearing. Then they were out of sight down the back side. I crawled out into the field. The grass was about three or four inches high and wet. I crawled for about twenty-five or thirty yards and looked around. I could see the machine gun that fired when the moon came out.

The clouds were racing across the sky blocking out the moon. It was blocked more often than shining.

I then spotted two men coming my way. They were talking more softly than the other ones were before. They passed by me not more than ten or fifteen feet away from me. They didn't see me. I thought if I am seen crawling around, they are going to think and might get suspicious. I got up slowly staying about twenty-five yards from the tree lines. I paralleled their lines. I kept mental notes of all the crew guns and about how many men they had. Then the woods stopped. The hill wrapped around to the right. Their lines stopped too. I stood there for a moment and followed the hill around to my right.

The moon came out for a few seconds. I could see the road in the valley below. I thought I would follow the hill to see if they had any reserves or mortars behind it. I cut back some toward the way I had come. I thought about what I would do. I thought, "I got away with murder so far. I might as well take a good look while I am here." I went to where I could see over the back side. I saw their mortars which were just barely out of sight on the back side of the hill. They were just far enough to be out of the grazing flat projectory fire.

I started to move to my left. I wanted to get back to the edge of the hill where there were no woods and no lines. I saw a man coming right at me. Behind him, I could see a tent with a light in it. It was just on the back side, out of sight of our lines. I started to walk the way I wanted to go. I figured the man would pass behind me.

He came up behind me and yelled something. I stopped and turned around. He was only a few steps away. He grunted something and pointed to a cigarette he had in his mouth. I had my rifle slung. I slipped my entrenching knife out of its case. I slowly walked toward him getting my cigarette lighter out. I walked up to him arm's length. He just stood there. The moon started to come out, and I stuck the lighter right under his cigarette and struck it. I lit his cigarette and started to back away. He grabbed my wrist. My left arm was fully extended by my left side. I raised it to about a forty-five degree angle of my body to the rear getting ready to thrust my knife in a rainbow motion. Just in time, I saw that he was only after my lighter. He took my lighter out of my hand, and it sounded like he started to chew me out. I turned and walked away. I took several steps and looked back over my shoulder. He was walking away. I called him a few choice names under my breath.

In the light of my lighter, I could see that he was a major. He didn't look like he was a full-blooded oriental. His eyes were only slanted half as much as the orientals. He had a dark complexion like he was part Polynesian.

I got to the edge of the hill. The moon had come back out, and I could see the road in the valley below. It was going in the right direction. I thought, "The hell with the swamps. I'll go back to the road." I was just starting to get dry and warm up some. I started down the hill toward the road. It reminded me of the country roads back home. Its base along the edge was large cobblestones with a finer chip surface. I walked slowly straight across it looking hard up and down. With the moon out, I could see a good way, and I saw nothing in either direction.

I slung my MI and started down the right berm. I was going at a slow but steady pace. I had gone about fifty or sixty yards when I pulled up sharply. I thought, "You stupid fool, there's sure to be a block on this road." I was looking for an easy way home and not thinking. I said to myself, "You're going to get yourself killed." I thought I must be pretty close to the halfway point between the two lines.

The next thought I had was, "Who's road block am I going to run into, ours or theirs?" I didn't care to run into ours as much as theirs because I was coming from the other side. I didn't pass through it on the way out. They wouldn't even know there was any GIs on this side. With me on this side, I thought they might get nervous and fire before they challenged. I just stood there pondering the situation. I looked at the shining still waters of the swamps and thought it might be a lot safer down there.

I continued down the right berm but much slower. I looked hard down the road ahead of me. Every several step, I would stop and look over the road to my rear. I didn't want anybody coming up behind me. It must have taken me fifteen minutes to go the next hundred yards. I was being much more careful. I must have gone forty or fifty yards farther when the moon came out, and I saw a bridge not too far ahead of me. I just stood there. I knew one side or the other would be holding it.

Again I looked at the cold waters of the swamp. The moon was reflecting off of it. I though it looked deep. It was so lazy and still. Just a few small ripples from the breeze that was blowing the clouds along. I thought how cold it would be down there.

Then a strange thing happened to me. I started to walk slowly. I didn't give my body any commands to go on. It was like a magnet was pulling me. I went four or five steps and stopped. I thought to myself, "What the hell's going on? Don't get careless now." I strained my eyes looking at the bridge. I could hardly make it, but now that the moon was behind a cloud, I stood there as beads of sweat started to form on my forehead. Then it happened again. I started to move toward the bridge. It was like I couldn't stop myself. I had no control. I remember telling myself, "You damn fool, you're going to get killed." I was about ten yards from the bridge when I stopped and stared across it. I could see nothing.

The bridge was a truss type. The trusses looked very sturdy. They looked as big as railroad ties. I thought it might support a tank. It looked about forty feet long. I just stood there frozen like a statue. I was still off on the right berm when the moon came out from behind a cloud once more, and I saw him standing on the far side against the left truss. He wasn't moving. He was just leaning against the truss, almost off the far end.

I thought he had to know I am here. It was walking on the chipped surface which was like walking on dry leaves. I thought, *Why isn't he challenging me?* Then another strange thing happened to me. I got goose bumps all over my back. Icy chills were running up and down my spine. The chills went down my arms to my fingertips and made them tingle. It felt like the hair on my head was standing straight up. I thought It must be some form of fear. Some men couldn't control their urine when they really got scared. I thought, "I'll take the easy way out. I'll let this guy have it." Then I thought, "If he is one of ours, I'll probably never be able to sleep again." I figured it was a fifty-fifty chance. I'll let him have it.

I slowly took several steps to the center of the road. At the same time, I was pulling my MI off my shoulder. I thought the only reason he isn't challenging me is because he is one of theirs, and I am coming from their side. I had my MI at arm's length. I turned my body, so it was pointed at him. The cold chills were still going up and down my back. The goose bumps felt like bug bites. It felt like electric going down my arms. I couldn't figure it out. I had my MI pointed at him now. I pushed the lock forward. It went with the distinctive click. I thought, "What the hell is he waiting for. He had to hear that." I slipped my finger back to the trigger. I aimed and pulled hard, and nothing happened. I pulled hard again and still nothing happened.

I staggered a few more steps toward the bridge and onto it. I was several steps on it when I stopped. I still had my MI pointed at him. I pulled the trigger again and still nothing happened. Sweat was running down my face. I thought this time I've had it. I thought about running and diving into the water and hiding under the bridge.

That strange force took over my body again. I took several more steps and stopped staring across the bridge at him. I thought I heard, "Is that you, Beaver?" I told myself, "You're hearing things." I thought I must have been in the first battalion sector. "No one even knows me there," I told myself. My hair was standing straight up on my neck. The chills were going wild. I walked three or four more steps and stopped again. I was sure then that I heard, "Is that you, Beaver?"

I answered softly, "Yeah."

I walked slowly across the bridge, and he waited for me on the far side. I saw who it was. It was Sergeant Altman. He lunged forward grabbing me and patting me on the back. He embraced me harder than I've ever been embraced. He picked me up and even swung me around. He started to shake me, and it sounded like he was going to cry when he said, "Boy, am I glad to see you. I never in my life was so glad to see someone like I am to see you." He kept telling me that I didn't know what he had been through and how glad he was.

He was getting loud, and I told him. "Damn it, sergeant, knock it off." We're not out of the woods yet. Then it happened. We got fired on from out of the swamp. We hit the deck of the bridge. I brought my MI up over the side of it and started to return the fire. I must have fired three clips. They finally stopped, and I told the sergeant, "Let's get the hell out of here."

We started down the road. We had gone a short ways when I stopped suddenly. I looked down at my MI, I thought, "What the hell's going on?" My MI wouldn't fire on the bridge, but it worked like a charm when we got fired on. Sergeant Altman asked me what was wrong. I said, "Nothing." I told the sergeant, "We must be in the Charlie company sector." We were going to be challenged pretty soon, and we don't know their sign.

All the time, I was thinking about what happened on the bridge. I was thinking about the chills and the tingling fingers. I was thinking about the goose bumps and losing control of my body and how it kept on going. Most of all, I was thinking about my MI not firing and a few seconds later working good.

We walked for a way. The road kept bearing to the right. When we got challenged, the sergeant answered, "We are two GIs from Easy company. We are coming in with weapons over our heads." They told us to come in. They took us to their company command post. The company commander came out and asked why we were here. We explained who we were and also told him we were coming back from patrol, and that we had to get to Easy company fast. He told his driver to get his jeep and take us over there.

All the way over, I couldn't forget what had happened. I thought we must have had some help from upstairs. It was the only explanation I could come up with. We got to the company command post. We thanked the driver for the ride. It was 0200 hours.

We went in to see the old man. He had the three green men sitting in there with him. I could tell by the look on their faces that they weren't enjoying it. He asked what we had found out. Sergeant Altman spoke right up. He told him that I was the only one to reach the enemy lines and said they had found out nothing unless I had. The captain looked at me. I told him that it was not Sergeant Altman's fault that he didn't reach their lines. I just turned around and looked at the green men. The captain glanced at them and looked back at me.

I told him how I reached their lines. I told him the green men had made a lot of noise and distracted them. I told him how I walked among them and showed him where their lines were along the tree line. I told him about the company's strength. I pointed out where their mortars were on the map and their command post. I said that I thought their mortars could be knocked out easily by our mortars.

He dismissed me but kept Sergeant Altman and the green men. As I left, I could hear him say, "What the hell went wrong with you and your men?"

I went outside and the first sergeant and the company executive officer was there. I told them I wanted to see the unit chaplain. The sergeant said, "Hell, man it's zero two twenty hours."

I said, "Damn it sergeant, a hell of a lot happened to me tonight. I got away with murder over there. I should be a dead man now." I thought the chaplain might want to see me. The executive officer told the sergeant to get the company driver and take me over there. The executive officer told me when I got back to sack out in the command post. He told me to sleep a little in the morning, and that I wouldn't have to take part in the attack.

When I got there, I told the driver to wait for me. I went into the chaplain's tent. There was an aid sleeping in front of the tent. I woke him and told him that I wanted to see the chaplain. He looked at his watch and said, "Do you know what time it is? Can't this wait until morning?"

I told him that I had been through a lot tonight, and I wanted to see the chaplain. I said, "I think he will want to see me." Just then the chaplain came in from the back of the tent. He wanted to know what all the noise was about. The aid explained and told him that he was trying to get me to wait until morning. The chaplain said, "I'm awake now. I will see him."

The chaplain was a big man. I would guess his age to be in his mid-thirties. He was stocky built. He looked like he weighed well over two hundred pounds.

I went into the back of the tent with him. He asked how he could help me. I explained what happened all the way through the patrol. He shunned it off and reassured me that everything would be all right. He told me everything was normal. All the way back, I couldn't get it out of my mind. I was really disappointed with the chaplain's explanation. I was sure we had gotten help from above.

We got back to the company and sacked out. I couldn't sleep. It kept going through my mind over and over. I thought about all the foolish and stupid things I had done with the airplane. I wondered if I were such a hotshot pilot, or if I had help from above.

The next thing I knew, I was awakened to the sound of distant shelling. I just lay there resting. I was trying to sort everything out in my mind when the shelling stopped. A few minutes later, the small arms fire started. It didn't last long, and it got very quiet. I thought the company must have taken the hill, or they would be back here with their tails between their legs by now. I also thought I had better get back to work or thinking about last night would drive me nuts.

I got up and went outside. The company weapons carriers were just getting ready to leave. I asked if I could hitch a ride. They said it was okay. I asked them to wait until I got my things. I doubled time to the squad area and got my things and ran back to the truck. They drove around the back side of our hill and got onto the road we were on last night. We went down the road and across the bridge. It gave me the willies. They stopped at the side of the hill. I got off. Just ahead of me were three jeeps and a two-and-a-half-ton truck. They had the prisoners there. They had a lot of them.

At the front of one of these jeeps was a captain from intelligence. He was questioning what looked like the major I ran into last night. I walked over, and before I got there, the executive officer joined the captain. The two officer were talking. Then they finished; the captain asked the enemy major something in Chinese. I waited until there was a pause in the conversation and said, "Excuse me, sir."

The company executive officer said, "What do you want, Beaver?"

I said, "I wonder if the captain would ask the major if I could please have my cigarette lighter back." They both looked at me like I was nuts. I said, "Please, sir, will you?" The captain thought a bit like he was trying to figure out how to say it. He then said something to the major in Chinese. The major turned to me with a frightened stare with his mouth wide open. He said something back to the captain.

The captain said, "He wants to know if that was you last night."

I said, "Tell him yes." The captain turned back to him and said one word. He talked again to the captain, and the captain looked at me. He had wanted to know how close to death he was last night. I looked at the major. He was looking at me in disbelief. His mouth was still wide open. I said, "Tell him that if he would have recognized me he would have died." The captain turned and told him. Beads of sweat started to form on the major's face as he reached into his pocket. He pulled out my lighter. He looked at it and handed it to me. I told the captain to thank him for me. He did, and the major said something to him. I looked at the captain.

He said, "Maybe I shouldn't tell you what he said." He leaned over and told the company executive officer.

The executive officer said, "Tell him he's a good man."

The captain said, "The major wants to know how they can win this war fighting with men with sure courage." I threw the enemy major a salute which he returned sharply. I told the captain to tell him that I wish him a good and long life.

As I walked away, I overheard the executive officer saying, "No damn wonder he wanted to see the chaplain last night." I walked away and hoped that what I said to the enemy major would ease his mind about being a prisoner. I had no doubt that he would be treated fairly.

As I walked toward the hill, someone yelled at me. I turned around and saw Sergeant Altman was coming at me in a trot. When he got to me he said, "I have to talk to you about last night and the bridge. I've got to tell you something. I couldn't sleep over it."

I said, "Hold it, sergeant. I think I know what you're going to say."

He said, "How do you know?"

I said, "Last night on the bridge, you tried to kill me, but your weapon wouldn't fire." He looked like the enemy major. His mouth was wide opened, and he was astonished.

He said, "How do you know that?"

I said, "Hell, sergeant. I tried to kill you, and my weapon wouldn't fire." I think his chin almost dropped to his chest. He started to stutter and finally got it out.

He said, "But you returned enemy fire we got."

I said, "Yes, Sergeant. I returned the fire."

He said, "How could you if your weapon wouldn't fire?"

I said, "Is that why you didn't fire?" He nodded his head and asked how it could have been. I just said, "I think we had some help. I think there was someone bigger than the two of us on that bridge last night."

I said to him, "Let me see your carbine." He told me that it wasn't the same one. He told me he had traded it for a new one this morning at the ordinance truck. There was an ordinance truck moving slowly through the parked vehicles. I ran over and stopped him. Sergeant Altman followed me. I asked the driver if he still had the sergeant's carbine and if he had done anything with it yet. He said that it was still in the rack where he put it. I asked if I could see it. He started to gripe. I said, "Please, it's important to me." He got out and went around to the back of the truck. He opened the door and brought the carbine back to me. I said, "Are you sure this is the one?" He had a few choice words for me.

As Sergeant Altman looked over my shoulder, he said, "That's it. It has my serial number on it." I asked the sergeant for a clip of ammo. He gave me one, and I put the weapon on semi-automatic. I pointed it at the ground about fifteen feet ahead of me and fired five or six rounds. I then put it on full automatic and fired off the rest of the clip. A lieutenant hollered to knock it off and stop firing around the prisoners.

I looked at Sergeant Altman. His mouth was wide open again. I lobbed the carbine at him, and as he caught it, I said, "Here, Sergeant. I would keep this weapon if I were you. It only shoots the bad guys."

We started up the hill exchanging notes from last night. I told him what happened to me on the bridge. He explained what happened to him. He said he felt like he was glued in that spot against the truss. He said when his carbine wouldn't fire he thought he was dead. I asked what the hell he was doing that far off our beat on the bridge. He told me, but I don't quite remember what the reason was. I asked, "Are you considering going to see the chaplain?" He said he had given it some thought. I told him to forget it. I told him that I was already there, and that I had got no satisfaction.

By this time, we were at the top of the hill. We got ready to go our own way when he said, "I owe you a lot." I told him that I would never forget him, or what had happened last night. He kept thanking me, and I told him that maybe he could do me a favor someday. He said, "Anytime, all you have to do is ask and it's yours." That was the last time I ever saw Sergeant Altman.

I found my squad and dug in. The weather was starting to warm up. We were there for a few days. The sun shown for several days, and it really warmed up. Some of the men laid around bare back trying to get a tan.

There was a lot of horse play going on. Some men throwing cold water on warm backs. Some practical jokes were being played also, but I tried to stay clear of it. One day, one was played on me, and I just had to laugh with the guys who did it.

A few of the men had ball gloves and a baseball. They were playing catch with it. Some of the men would even find something to use for a bat. They would try to use big sticks which would break with the first hit of the ball. I still wonder where the hell they got the ball and gloves.

4

ON ONE OF THESE NICE sunny mornings, the first sergeant came early to each platoon. He said he needed men for detail. He was in the second platoon saying that he wanted eleven men. He came over to the first and wanted nine men and a non-commissioned officer. The platoon sergeant asked if I would mind going. I didn't know what the detail was, but I thought it would be something to do, and so I took it.

I reported to the company command post. There were thirty-three men there and myself. The first sergeant told me to take them and report to battalion command post. I thought this detail was getting interesting and wondered what it was.

When I arrived at the battalion, there were already about fifty or sixty men there. The battalion sergeant major came out and looked us over. He asked, "Where the hell is the officer from Fox company?" There was no response. He then asked, "Where is the non-commissioned officer from easy company?"

I said, "Here."

He said, "Front and center." I went up with him. He called the noncommissioned officer from George company. Again there was no answer. The sergeant looked at me and said, "Have you ever been in charge of ninety-three men in detail?"

I said, "No, Sergeant."

He replied, "You are now. Come on inside."

I went in with him thinking what this could be all about. We got inside, and there were three lieutenants and the battalion commander waiting for us. They were looking over a large map. The battalion commander turned to the sergeant and asked, "Where is the officer?"

The sergeant answered. "None were sent over, sir." He then asked for the ranking non-commissioned officer. The sergeant pointed at me and said, "This is him. He is the only non-commissioned officer that was sent over, sir." The battalion commander looked very displeased. I wondered what the hell I had got myself into.

He called me over to the map and pointed to a hill. He said, "This hill has no military value to us, but if the enemy was to put an observation post on it, they would be able to see everything we do. We've got to get a unit put on it. We are going to send this detail there until we can get a unit from reserves to occupy it." It was marked, "Hill 427."

He said, "I'm going to send one of my aids with you to help you get set up. I'm also going to send with you ammo and supply for the outfit that relieves you. You will be relieved no later than noon tomorrow. Be ready to leave in one hour."

I went outside and informed the men what was going on. I told them to go back to their company and get ready. I also told them to be prepared to stay overnight and be back within an hour.

All the way back to the company, I kept asking myself. "What did I get myself into now?" They called it detail. I thought I was going to be in charge of some kind of work crew. I started to tell myself, "Maybe we will just go up there and spend the night nicely and peacefully and come back in time for noon chow tomorrow." This was not to be.

I got back to the company. I rolled up my bed roll and got a fresh canteen of water. I filled up my ammo belt while getting a lot of rousing from the squad for volunteering. I told them. "When I volunteered, I didn't know 'detail' was another name for patrol." The hour was about up. I had to take off for battalion. I said my farewells to the squad, and they wished me good luck. I didn't know it then, but it was to be the last time I was ever to see them. They were all damn good men. I would have shared my shelter with anyone of them anyplace in the world.

When I arrived back at the battalion, most of the men were already there. A young second lieutenant was in a jeep with a trailer on it full of ammo and supplies. There was also a large radio we were taking also, "We finally got arranged and started out. The young lieutenant and the jeep were in the lead. It took the best part of an hour to get to the hill. It wasn't that it was so far away, but we had to go the only way the jeep could go. I guess we were about a mile or a mile and a half from the company to the northwest.

The hill looked easy to defend. A large creek wound about half-way around it. The west side was very steep. It was not impossible for anyone to come up that way but very unlikely. The east side was wide open. There was no cover or protection of any kind. I didn't think we would get any trouble from there. They would catch hell if they tried that way. It would be almost suicide to come that way. The north side was the most likely place trouble would come from. The lieutenant and I placed the men from the west around to the east. There was about eighty percent of our fire power facing the north slope. We had two light thirties. We set them up to have interlocking fire on the north slope. The one on the left could turn and cover the east slope if necessary. We spaced our BARs (Browning Autograph Rifles) evenly between them. We filled the line with MIs. We put a squad of MI's on the east slope and told them if they started to fire, we would get some help to them. We then sent several men to the west slope to keep an eye on it. We didn't expect to see any trouble coming from there.

The north slope was fairly steep near the top and went into a gentle slope the rest of the way down to the road at the bottom. The road went around the bottom along the north side to the west side, across the bridge and out of our sight on the west side. The north side was partly wooded. It had a few gullies where troops could take shelter from our fire. We had one mortar, and we set it up to cover them. We had three details to dig holes near the top to put our ammo and supplies in them. We didn't want to put all of our eggs in one basket.

The men started to dig in. It was about mid-morning when I noticed the young lieutenant was not digging. I said, "Sir, you should at least dig a slit trench to sit in."

He replied, "I will as soon as you get dug in and ready to my satisfaction. I'm going back." We were about halfway dug in when one of the outpost came in. We put an outpost about one hundred and fifty yards out. He was in front of our lines on the north slope.

He told us that there was an enemy patrol coming across the bridge. The lieutenant and I agreed to let them go by if they weren't coming up here. We ordered all the men out of sight. He thought the longer we went unnoticed up here, the better it would be. They soon came in sight. The lieutenant put his glasses on them. He said quietly to me, "I don't think they are going by. It looks like an observation team and a squad of infantry." They went on down the road fifty or sixty yards from the bridge and started up the slope. It was about three hundred and fifty yards from our position. We let them come for about a hundred yards or so, and the lieutenant ordered about a dozen men to fire, so they would not know our strength on the hill. They opened up on them. I saw several of them drop. The rest of them went running back where they came from.

The lieutenant got on the radio and reported the action to the battalion. He told them what we had been up against and also that the enemy had a few casualties, and we had none.

About half an hour later, I noticed the lieutenant was sitting under a tree. He was looking at some charts and fooling with a clip board. I was just going to tell him that he may as well go back now that we were dug in and ready for just about anything they could hit us with. We had one mortar, two light thirties, and a half dozen or so BARs, and one hell of a lot of MIs. I thought we would have no trouble holding the hill against a company of the enemy.

Just then all hell broke loose. Mortar shells started coming in everywhere. They must have had the hill zeroed in because they were right on target. We caught hell for several minutes, when we found out that there was about a platoon of enemy about halfway up the hill. I started to fire on them, and the rest of the so called detail opened up too. They retreated back down the hill suffering heavy casualty, at least 50 percent.

I turned to the lieutenant. He was dead. The radio had had it too. I went around the lines checking for casualties. We had some wounded from the shelling but nothing serious. I made up squads and appointed squad leaders. The medic was attending to the wounded. I told the two appointed squad leaders on the light thirties that if they were to lose a man from anything, they were to get one from one of the rifle squads. I also told the men as I went around that I didn't know what they would do next, or if they would do anything at all. I said, "They took a pretty good licking on the first two tries. I hope they have had enough." It depended on how badly they wanted this hill. I told them to stay in their holes as much as possible. We didn't know when we were going to be hit with mortars again.

It was mid-afternoon, and I looked at the dead lieutenant lying under the tree, and then I looked at the battered up radio. I thought how easy it would be if it were working. I also thought that maybe the battalion would think something was wrong when the lieutenant didn't show back up there. Then it hit me. The lieutenant's jeep was parked just over the hill out of sight.

I called the private back to my hole. I explained what I wanted him to do. I wanted him to take the lieutenant's jeep and go back to the battalion. I said, "Tell them that the lieutenant is dead, and that we're catching hell up here. Tell him that we also have casualties, and that if the shelling and attacks get heavier, I don't know how long we can hold." We both doubled time to the top and over the back of the hill. There was the jeep parked under a tree. It had had it. It didn't take a hit, but it looked like a sieve from a few near misses. We weren't going anywhere in it. I then asked the private if he could remember what I told him, or if he wanted me to write it down for him. He said he had no trouble remembering what had happened here. I then sent him on foot back to the battalion.

Upon returning to my position, I noticed the ammo bearers for the light thirties carrying extra cans of ammo back to their guns. They must have thought as I did. The enemy wanted this hill so badly they would try twice in such a short time to get it. I thought that a major attack was sure to come. They were probably getting set up for it right now. I thought that if a major attack did come, battalion would surely hear it. I thought that the runner should be getting back in a half an hour or forty-five minutes. Give battalion fifteen or twenty minutes to get together as a unit and another thirty or forty-five minutes to get here. I thought that if we could hold for two hours, we would be all right. Once again, I was wrong in my thinking.

About an hour went by and nothing happened. I was beginning to think, *We might be all right, and that battalion was probably on their way.* When in came the mortars, again they were right on target. I squated down in my hole holding my ears and opening my mouth. This relieved the deafening sounds of the mortar shells exploding. They kept coming for what seemed like five minutes. I knew the enemy infantry was moving up the hill as close as they dared to get to the shelling. Soon, the shelling would move back to about the top of the hill allowing them to get closer and us to start firing. I could hear it slowly climbing up the hill until it was all behind us.

I got up and saw the enemy. I thought this was it. The enemy infantry was all over the hill. There was a company, or better, we started firing. I signaled the mortars to start firing. We had one hell of a fire fight for a few minutes with the enemy suffering heavy casualty. They began to pull back. We kept our fire on them, and they moved their mortars back on us. We had to pull in our necks. This allowed them to retreat without any harassment. The shelling soon stopped, and I yelled from my hole to the squad leaders for a casualty report. Each one yelled back their report, and I tallied it up. We had nine men wounded and four dead. I said to myself, "That makes a total of thirteen wounded and five dead."

I looked over the front. I could see some enemy wounded moving and hear some moaning. I just stared out at them and went into a semitrance. I could see the fighting going on all over again. The screams of the men getting hit on both sides was echoing through my head. It's an indescribable scream. You can almost tell if the man was dead, dying, or if he's going to pull through it.

I came out of the trance quickly when my eye caught some movement at the bottom of the hill. I got my glasses out to take a good look at it. It was a team of enemy medic moving up the hill.

I raised up some out of my hole. I said, "There is a team of enemy medics moving up the hill, and they are not to be fired on."

I watched them make their way up to where the wounded and the dead were. They started to go from body to body. One of them made his way fifty or sixty yards directly out in front of me where he found a wounded man and started to work on him. He was there for several minutes when I raised up about halfway out of my hole. He stood straight up and took a half step backward like he didn't know what to do. I made a gesture with my hand for him to go back to work and that I wasn't going to bother him. He nodded his head and did so.

I watched him for five or ten minutes with him looking up at me several times. I tried to smile at him one time he looked at me, and I crawled back into my hole.

It was late afternoon, and I tried to think of what they would do next. I put myself in their place. I thought of the west side. I told myself no then thinking a man would have to be part mountain goat to come up there, plus get fired on. I counted that out but sent a man around to the two men watching it and told them to be on their toes anyway.

I thought of the east side next and then ruled it out too. They would be wide open over there and catch hell. I also considered the north side, and then I told myself, "If they come again, it will be from the same place."

Then I thought, "What will they try next?" I put myself in their place again. If I wanted this hill and got the hell beat out of me trying to get it. what would I do? "I surely wouldn't want to try another frontal attack. I would try to get a tank or two. What the hell would we do if they hit us with a tank or two?" We had no way of stopping them. We would have to get the hell out of here and fast. A tank would cut us up pretty good before we could get over the top of the hill. I also thought that they might not have any available.

Another hour and a half went on. It was early evening. I thought they would try again before dark. I told myself, "They may even be waiting for tanks." I went to each squad leader and told them. Just before dark, I wanted each of them to send some men down the hill to set up trip wires and booby trap them with grenades. I told them to use boot laces if they had to. I wanted all they could rig all over the north side.

I then went back to my hole, and I caught my breath. I wondered if they would try at night and how hard. I went back to the mortar position. I asked them to see if there were any flares in any of the ammo pits for their gun. I said, "If there is, they were to fire one anytime they thought it was necessary or on my command." I told them, "If there were no flares, they were to use white phosphorus." I said, "If one of those trip wires go off, get one up fast, and if we get an attack, keep the front lit as best you can."

I went back to my hole. As I approached it, I could see the men setting up their trip wires. They were covering the slope well. If an attack came, we would know about it before they get on us.

After they were done with the north side, I walked over to the east slope and had them do the same. I thought there might be a chance they would try this side at night. I left there and went to the men on the west slope. I didn't expect any trouble to be coming from there. I told them to rig a few on the most likely avenue of approach.

I noticed one of the ammo bearers for the mortar. He looked young. I was twenty-one at the time, and he looked three or four years younger than I was. He looked really frightened. He was scared half to death. I walked over to him. I said to him, "I guess I am as scared as you look."

He said, "You mean you're scared too?"

I said, "You're damn right. I'm scared. Everybody here is scared, and if anybody tells you he isn't, he's a damn liar. I'm always afraid. If there is nothing to be afraid of at the present, I'm afraid of what tomorrow might bring." I patted him on the shoulder and said, "Hang in there, boy. You'll be all right."

I then thought about the outpost. I went back to the ammo pits and found a flare gun and five or six flares. I took it to the outpost and gave it to them. I told them if they hear anything to fire one. I told them that they would be relieved every two hours, and that they were to pass that order along.

As I went back to my hole, I looked at the sky. I remembered telling myself that it would be dark in less than an hour. I wandered what they were up to. They had plenty of time to organize another attack. We're they waiting for darkness? I thought, "If they are, we're ready as we ever will be for them."

As I looked over the north slope, I noticed most of the men that were setting trip wires were back. I crawled into my hole and sat on the firing step. As I sat there, I asked myself over and over again what they were going to do. I tried to outguess them. I thought about sending a runner back, but I scratched that idea. It would be dark in fifteen or twenty minutes. He might get lost or shot trying to cross our lines. I could have kicked myself for not doing it earlier.

As I sat there thinking, in came the mortars right on target again. They pounded us for four or five minutes. When they stopped, I got up ready to start firing, but there were no enemy troops assaulting us. We could see for about one hundred to one hundred and fifty yards. There was nothing. I called for the mortar to send up a flare. When they did, it lit the whole north slope. There was nothing again. This kept up all through the night at least once an hour with no certain timing. After each shelling, we sent up a flare but not once did they attack. But I knew we had some wounded from the night shelling. Several times through the night, I heard those screams.

The eastern sky started to brighten. Dawn was coming, and I wondered if they would hit us at dawn, and if I should send back another runner. I kept hearing the battalion commander saying, "You will be relieved tomorrow no later than noon." I wondered if it would be worth it. I thought I'd wait and see what the dawn brought up.

I went around to check each squad and pep them up. The night shelling took its toll. We had two more dead and five wounded. This made a total of seven dead and eighteen wounded. The less seriously wounded were still manning their weapons. I went back to my hole. I could see fairly good now. The sun looked like it was trying to pierce the hill to our east; its rays were coming over the hill. I just sat there with a wait and see attitude.

It was about a half an hour later when the mortars came in again. This time they kept up for about ten minutes. We raised our firing. They were about one hundred and fifty yards away, and there was well over a company of them. We had another hell of a fire fight with them. They got within one hundred yards of our position before withdrawing. Their casualties were very heavy again. I couldn't find ours out. As soon as they were down the hill, the shelling started again. It was much lighter this time but steady. It was just enough to keep us pinned in our holes. It kept up for an hour and then into two hours. I wondered what they were up to, or what they thought that they were gaining by it.

It must have been near mid-morning. I was contented to set out the shelling until noon when our relief would arrive. They wouldn't let me have it that way. The shelling started to intensify. They poured it on again. It kept up for about ten or fifteen minutes. They were giving us hell. I heard some of our men yelling, but I couldn't make out what they were saying. Then I heard some firing, and it was from our guns. I raised my head up enough to see. The enemy infantry was almost upon us. They looked like they were walking right into their own mortar barrage. I started to yell to the men who didn't know it yet to get up and start firing. I was firing and yelling and our firing started to pick up. The enemy troops were getting dangerously close. I started to yell as hard as I could to get my voice above the noise of the mortars exploding. I was firing as fast as I could when I got a stinging and numbing sensation over the right side of my body from the waist up. I wondered what the hell it was when I felt blood running down my neck onto my shoulder. I then felt it running down my sideburn and onto my cheek. I wiped it off and looked at it. It made me mad. I raised my rifle to continue firing when my knees started to buckle. I got very dizzy, and I dropped to my knees wondering how bad it was. I had no pain. Then I thought of the man talking about it. They had said the ones you don't feel are the bad ones. I tried to get up, and I must have passed out.

I don't know how long I was out, but when I awoke, the mortars were still coming in, and the firing was still heavy. I made it to my feet. I looked over the front. Some enemy took cover where they could be covering fire for the ones still trying to overrun us. I thought of the secondary position. We could fall back there near the top of the hill. Our position would be tighter together with less area to defend. I got up out of the hole and started yelling, "Fall back to the secondary position." I yelled it two or three times and turned to run to them. I took four or five steps, and that's all I remember.

I don't know how long I was out again, but when I awoke, I only came out of it about seventy-five percent of the way. I knew that I was lying face down, and someone was holding on my back. I also noticed that the mortars had stopped and small arms firing was heavy near what must have been the top of the hill. It must have been coming from our secondary position. I wondered who in the hell stayed back with me.

I passed out, and once again, I don't know for how long. I woke as I was being rolled over. I opened my eyes and got the shock of my life. I either passed out or fainted when I saw what I saw. The person working on me was an enemy medic. I awoke and opened my eyes and looked at him. He must have sensed that I was awake. He stopped working on my legs and turned and looked at me. When our eyes met, I could see in his eyes the deepest look of compassion as if he were trying to tell me. "Don't worry. I'm not going to harm you. I'm only trying to help you." He looked at me for just a moment and went back to work on my legs.

I lay there looking up at the sky. The firing was still heavy near the top of the hill. I wondered how long they could hold. It wasn't long until I started to hear choppers. It sounded like they were all around us. They must have been landing on the back side of the hill.

The firing soon got heavier along with some screaming. The enemy started retreating back down the hill. I saw several go by us. Then several minutes later, I saw some of our troops go by. The enemy medic paid no attention to either. He just kept working on my legs.

Just about then, a man of Spanish decent from Easy company first platoon, whom I knew quite well, walked up to me. He knelt down on his knees beside my head. He gently took my head and cradled it on his lap. He then reached down and gently tugged on my shoulders saying, "Sergeant Beaver, Sergeant Beaver." I didn't answer him. I just looked into his eyes. He got a frightened look on his face. He looked up the hill and screamed for a medic.

He then put my head gently back on the ground. The enemy medic never paid any attention to him. He just kept on working on me. He then stood up, turned, and looked down the north slope. He then said with a Spanish accent. "You son of a bitches, if I get you, I will kill you. All of you." He started to walk away. As he did, he muttered, "That doesn't go for you, medic." I don't think I will ever forget him.

A team of medics soon got to me. They almost had to force the enemy medic off of me. He kept talking to them like he was telling them what he had done and what needs to be done.

The one medic said, "What the hell is he talking about? Let's get the interpreter down here." I asked how bad I was. He said, "Both of your legs have been hit pretty badly. You have one in your hip, one in the back, one in the right arm, one in the neck, and one in your head." He continued, "I don't like the look of your neck and head. We will get you out of here as soon as the plasma is in you."

The interpreter soon got there. Colonel Woods, the battalion commander, was with him. Colonel Woods came over to me. He knelt down over me. His eyes filled with water as he looked at me as if he were apologizing for not getting there sooner. He said, "Your runner was found by Charlie company this morning. He was pretty badly wounded, but he's going to be all right. We got here as soon as we could once we got the word. Is there any pain, sergeant?"

I muttered, "No, sir."

He then went back to the interpreter. He told the colonel that the enemy medic wanted to evacuate me to his aid station, which wasn't very far away. He said I would receive proper treatment there. The colonel said, "Like hell, this man isn't a prisoner of war. He will evacuate through our channels."

By this time, they were putting me on a litter getting ready to get me out of there. I motioned for Colonel Woods to come to me. He did and knelt over me. I said, "Sir, I would consider it a personal favor if you would let the enemy medic return to his own lines if he wants to go. He stayed and worked on me for a good while." He nodded his head in agreement. I nodded mine in a gesture of thanks. I then asked him if he would thank him for me.

They picked me up then and started up the hill. 'We went by the man of Spanish decent. He had his back to me. I heard him say to the men he was talking to as they carried me by, "Boy, you should have seen Sergeant Beaver. He was just one bloody mess."

As they carried me up the hill, I thought, "This sure is a strange war I got myself hooked up in. First, we try like hell to kill one another and then go out of our way to help one another."

They carried me over the hill and to a waiting chopper. They strapped me onto it. They already had a litter on the other side. As soon as they got me strapped in, the chopper took off.

It seemed like only a minute or two until we were landing. I was carried into a large tent. I was in battalion aid station. They put me on a table with huge lights hanging over me. Two teams of doctors started to work on me.

They numbed my legs and started to probe for schrap metal. They didn't get any out of my legs. They told me it would probably never bother me anyways. They said, "Let's get them sewed up." When they were about halfway done, they ordered a blood count. A nurse took some blood out of me. Then a few minutes later, she put a whole pint of blood into me. Then an older doctor looked at my head and neck. He had a nurse clean them while the other doctors got schrap metal out of my hip and back. They had a hard time with my right arm. They worked for quite a while on it. Then they finally got a piece of schrap metal out of it. They sewed it up. The older doctor then came back. While looking at the head and neck wound, he said to the other doctors, "I think we had better send him back to division. They are better equipped to handle this." He looked down at me and said, "Do you hear me?"

I muttered, "Yes, sir."

He then patted me on the shoulder and said, "You're going to be all right, son."

I lay there for several minutes. The nurse unplugged the blood. It was all in me. I was beginning to feel a little stronger. I was getting my wits about me when I heard a chopper landing close by. Soon two men took me to the chopper. This time I was on a litter and put inside. The chopper took-off. I was the only patient on board. There was one medic. He sat up front near the pilot. I noticed him looking back at me every minute or two. After what seemed to be a twenty or thirty-minute flight, we landed. I was carried into another tent. They put me on another table with huge lights over it.

I had no sooner than got on the table when they wheeled a portable x-ray machine over me, so the men started to take x-rays. They took four or five of them then took the machine and left.

Soon a team of three doctors and two nurses gathered around me. One of the doctors had the x-rays. He put them on a rack in front of a light and looked them over. After a few minutes of discussion, one of them came over to me and sat down beside me. He looked at me and asked if I could hear him. I was feeling a little better and said, "Yes, sir."

He said, "Boy, you're really quiet for as alert as you are."

I said, "I don't feel much like talking or have anything to say."

He said, "If I were you, I would have a lot of questions to ask."

I said, "I think you guys know what you're doing."

He said, "I wish everyone felt like you. From the chatter on the radio, you guys really gave them hell up there."

I said, "Yes, sir, and we got a little too." He then left and went back to the other doctors.

They talked some more over the x-rays, and he walked back over to me. He looked down at me and said, "The piece in your neck. We're not going to bother with. It's a very small piece, and we don't think it will ever bother you where it is, but the one in your head has to come out." He told me I had a very bad concussion and used some medical word for it that I can't remember. He told me they were going to take it out right now.

The nurses moved several trays of instruments around me and placed a towel over my head. I heard one of them say, "You're going to feel a pinch in your hip." I did, and it was the last thing I remembered until I started waking up. I heard another voice say, "Try to lay as still as you can." I tried to move my hand to feel my head, and I heard the voice say again. "Lie perfectly still. This is very important." I didn't get my wits about me for a day or two. I remember nurses coming and checking my temperature, pulse, and blood pressure.

I started to ask questions for the first time. I asked how bad I was. The nurses told me that the worst was my right arm and my head. She said, "As soon as your lacerations heal, they will be all right. I think your head wound is your million-dollar baby." I know I smiled. I should have if I didn't.

I was bandaged from my knees to the top of my head. My right arm was in a sling and bandaged to my chest. I asked if it was broken, and the answer was no. They told me that they put it that way to demobilize it, so I wouldn't move it so much.

I got the daily routine which was a change of bandages, a shot or two, and a few pills. On one of the rounds the nurse said to me, "I don't want to get your hopes up, but I think I overheard the doctors talking about you. I think I heard the name of Walter Reed mentioned."

The next day the doctor checked me over and said, "How would you like to go home?"

I said, "That would be great." He told me all I needed was a lot of rest and rehabilitation.

The doctor said, "I might as well tell you. Your right eye is damaged, and to what extent, we don't know. They can check it out in the states. It may not be much, but it could be. I just think you ought to know." He then asked, "What hospital would you like to go to?"

I said, "The only one I can think of close to home is Walter Reed."

He said, "That's funny. I think I saw that name on your orders." He told me it would probably be a day or two before I left.

That night I couldn't sleep. I kept thinking of home. They were probably getting worried about me. I couldn't write with my right arm in a sling, and every time I thought about it, everyone around me seemed too busy.

It started raining really hard, and I thought about my squad. I wondered what they were doing to keep dry. I also wondered if anyone was on patrol. I really felt sorry for them and thought of how many would make it and how many would end up like me.

The next morning, two nurses changed my bandages. They replaced most with large band aids except for my arm and head. My head was completely bandaged except for my mouth, the end of my nose and my left eye. They joked with me and told me they were wrapping me and ready to ship. I asked them if I was leaving today. They said, "You sure are. You are going to be busy until you leave which won't be long."

The doctor came in to see me. He said, "You are leaving as soon as I can okay it." He checked me all over and said, "I can't find any reason to keep you. So you are on your way."

I got to Walter Reed eight days after I was hit. I stayed in Japan one day and then went to Hawaii for a day, overnight in San Francisco, and on to Walter Reed.

While I was in Hawaii, an incident happened I think I should mention. I got there early in the morning and was met by an ambulance. It wasn't just me. The plane was full of wounded GIs and men rotating. I was taken to a military hospital and was given a complete check-up. They gave me the okay to go on, but they couldn't get me on a military plane. The head nurse told me not to worry about it. She said that she knew some of the nurses were going to the states later on that evening, and she would see if they would look after me. She must have had some pull because she got me on a commercial fight and got the okay for the nurses to accompany me.

That evening I was taken by ambulance to Honolulu airport. They didn't take me into the main terminal, but I was wheeled on a litter into a side door and down a hall. They took me into a room that looked like a waiting room and parked me along a wall.

A few feet across the aisle, there were people seated. I think they were waiting for a flight. I noticed this older lady looking at me. I would guess her to be in her late sixties. Every time I looked her way, she was staring at me. I must have been a sight all bandaged up like I was. I looked at her again, and her eyes were filled with tears. It looked like her heart was going to come right out for me.

I said softly, "Don't worry about me, ma'am. I will be all right." She got up and came over to me. She reached across me and took my hand; it was the only thing that wasn't bandaged on top of the blankets. She was staring down at me when an orderly came and wheeled me away. As I left, she said, "Put your trust in him, son, and you will be all right." By this time, I was several feet away. I said, "If you only knew how much trust I had in him."

She came back in a louder voice, "That's it, son. Keep your faith, and you'll be all right." I don't think. I will never forget her either.

Like I said, I got to Walter Reed eight days after I was hit. I arrived about 11:00 in the morning. By the time, I was put through the mill it was 5:00 p.m. A nurse brought me a tray. She said that she had kept it as warm as she could. I asked her if she got time if she would write a couple letters for me. I said, "It's been almost a month since my wife and family have heard from me."

She came right back with, "I will not. There is talk that you're going to get the VIP treatment. It looks like they're going to make a big fuss over what you did." Well, that was all I heard of that. It must have been just talk. She then said, "I think the government owes you a couple of phone calls. I will get a phone in here for you."

It was about an hour later when a man in what looked like a maintenance uniform came in. He hooked up the phone by my bed. Before he got it hooked up, the nurse came back and checked to see if it was working. She then asked for the names, addresses, and the numbers of the calls I wanted to make. I gave her my wife's first and then my mother and father's next. She got the long distance operator and handed me the phone.

I could hear the operator getting the local operator and giving her the numbers. I heard a busy signal. The operator on my end said that the line was busy. She said, "Do you want a second call or do you want to cut in?"

I said, "Would you please cut in?" I heard the operator saying to the other operator that this was going to be a government priority call and to cut in. I heard her cutting in and telling the number I was calling to hang up, and that she had a government priority call for it. I heard my wife's sister saying, "Quick, get Dolores," before she hung up. A few minutes later, I heard the phone ring, and the operator asking for Mrs. Dolores Beaver. A few seconds later, I heard her say, "Hello."

I choked up and said, "Is that you Dee?"

She said, "Yes, who is this?"

I said, "It's your husband." Everything got quiet. I said hello several times, but there was no response. Her older sister came to the phone then and said that Dolores was unable to talk and asked if she could take any messages.

I said, "Tell her I will call her back in twenty to thirty minutes."

She asked, "Who is this?"

I said, "Your brother-in-law."

She said, "'Who?"

I said, "It's Dolores's husband."

I heard her say. "My god." She came back then and said Dolores was sitting there crying her eyes out. I told her to try and calm her down, and that I would call back as soon as I called my mother.

I told the operator to get my second call, but when I was done, I wanted the first number again. Shortly, I heard the phone ring, and my mother said, "Hello." The operator asked for Mr. or Mrs. Harry Beaver. I heard her say, "I'm Mrs. Beaver," The operator told her to go ahead.

I said, "Hello, Mom."

I got the same question, "Who is this?"

I said, "It's your son. Jack."

She said, "Oh, wait a minute." I heard her going to the door and calling dad. He was probably working in the garden or the yard. She came back to the phone and said, "Where are you?" I told her that I was at the Walter Reed hospital near the District of Columbia. I then heard her tell dad that it was me on the phone. He wouldn't talk because he was hard of hearing. We talked for nearly a half an hour. I had to tell them every nick and scratch I had and how good they were taking care of me. I told mom to tell dad that they better have a good deer hunt planned for next season, and that I would probably be home, with a promise to write as soon as I could. I hung up. I told the operator that I wanted the first call back, and that I would talk to whoever answers.

The phone rang, and Dee's sister answered. I asked if Dee was able to talk now. She just said, "It's for you, Dolores."

The next thing I heard was Dee saying, "Yes," I asked if she was able to talk now and she said, "Yes." She asked the same question, "Where are you?" I answered all her questions, and she asked how bad I was.

I said, "That's one thing I want to talk about. We've been married for almost a year now, and we've only seen one another for about two weeks of that time." I offered, "Maybe you want out of it."

She came back with, "Do you?"

I answered, "No."

She said, "What would make you think that I would want out of it?"

I said, "When you married me, you married a whole man, and when I come back, I might be only half a man."

She said, "I'll take whatever is left." She asked again about how bad I was.

I told her, "I've got five pieces in my right leg, six in my left leg, one in my right hip, one in my back, one in my neck, one in my right arm, and one in my head."

She said, "What did they do? Did they put you up against the wall and use you for target practice?"

We talked for a while when her brother-in-law wanted to know where I got it at. I told her to tell him on hill 427. He said, "That hill made TV news. It had said that there was some fierce fighting going on there, and that the casualties were high on both sides. I wondered how many we had lost and if the hill was worth it."

I thought, "Maybe I should have got those men the hell out of there." I wondered if I would ever find out.

I heard Dee saying, "Are you still there?"

I said, "Yes, I was just thinking." She asked about what I told her I was just wondering if the hill was worth it. I explained to her that I was in charge on that hill, and that I was wondering if I had done the right thing. I said, "All of those casualties are on my shoulders." I told her I didn't want to talk about it anymore, and that I would write to the squad to find out as soon as they took my arm out of the harness they had it in.

We talked for about an hour. I told her that we had better hang up. I said, "I'll probably get a good night's sleep tonight." I gave her my address and promised to write or call as soon as I could. I explained that I didn't know when I could do either. I wasn't allowed out of bed yet. We hung up, and I did get a good night's sleep. I think it was the first time I slept straight through the night without waking up four or five times for a long time.

I later found out that after we hung up the phone, Dee went over and cried on her mother's shoulder and said, "He thinks that I won't want him because he got all shot up."

The next morning, I went through the usual routine. After dinner, things quieted down and got back to normal. I was lying on my bed trying to read a sporting magazine. It was hard to hold and turn the pages with just one hand. It seemed to tire me out, trying to read with one eye. I soon gave it up. I noticed that some of the guys in the ward were getting some visitors, and I thought that I would try to get some sleep.

I turned on my side and a nurse came in. She was making the bed next to me. It was the same one that got the phone for me. I asked her if she had got in trouble over it yet. She said, "No, it wasn't the first time it had been done." I thanked her again for doing it. We started to gab about the usual things, and I asked her if she knew when I would be allowed out of bed. She said that it would be up to the doctor. She didn't have any idea when it would be.

Just then, I saw a visitor coming down the ward, in a reflection in the window. It was a young girl. I thought that she resembled Dee a lot. The reflection passed the window, and I forgot about it. A few seconds later, she walked past the foot of my bed. I looked down at her. It was Dee. She was walking by me looking from side to side and bed to bed. She was about one bed from me when I said, "Dee." The nurse was bent over making the bed, and she looked up at me like I was crazy and saw I was looking by her. She turned, and by this time, Dee was starting toward me. The nurse stepped in front of her and said, "Now wait a minute. He has a very bad concussion. So take it easy." Then she stepped away.

Dee came over to me and bent down over me. She stayed there for a few seconds. I reached up with my left arm and put it around her. I pulled her toward me, and we kissed. I could feel a tear running down my face. I pushed her away a little and looking in her eyes I said, "The worst is behind us, and I'm home to stay." By this time, the nurse brought her a chair, and I asked her what she was doing here. She just said, "You are here, aren't you?" I asked her how she had got here. She told me that her mother, sister, brother, and brother-in-law came down. She told me that they would only let her in here to see me. She stayed all afternoon and then left to get a bite to eat. She came back about 6:30 and told me that they were going to stay the weekend. It was Thursday. I told her, "Maybe I can see your family before they go home." She stayed until eight o'clock when they were to pick her up. She asked when she was leaving if she could get me anything for tomorrow. I said, "Yeah, how about a thirty, day leave." A little smile came over her face, and she said, "Oh boy."

On her way out, I saw her stop a ward nurse. She talked to her for about fifteen minutes. I don't know what about I never asked.

I later found out that Dee's mother waited up that night of the phone calls for Dee's brother to come home from work. He worked second shift at a local plant. He got home about midnight. When he got home, Dee's mother told him about the phone calls and everything that happened.

5

She stared at him for a few minutes. He just said, "Is first thing in the morning soon enough?" She nodded her head, and he went out and got his car serviced and gassed up at a nearby twenty-four-hour gas station.

The next morning, Dee's mother woke her up. She got up and said, "What are you getting me up so early for. It's still dark out."

Her mother said, "You want to leave early don't you?" Dee jumped out of bed and hugged her and thanked her.

When Dee returned the next day, she seemed concerned about my head. She started to ask questions about it. I told her that it was the only thing keeping me here. All the other wounds didn't hit a vital part of me or even a bone. They were just about healed up. I said, "The one in my arm must have torn it up, or they would have had it out of this by now." I also told her that they made no promises on my right eye. They said, it could be blind or normal, and they wouldn't know until it healed.

That day, we both talked to the nurse to try to get the rest of the relations in. She wouldn't make any promises. We told her how far they had come, and that I would really like to see them.

The next day, Dee came right after dinner. She was there for about an hour when in came the rest of them. After the usual greetings and questions, they told me they were only allowed to stay for a half an hour. After their visit was up, which I enjoyed very much, the nurse asked them to leave. Dee decided to go with them to get something to eat. As they were leaving, I called Dee's brother-in-law back in. I asked, "That news you saw on TV about hill 427 did it give the number of casualties we had?"

He said, "No, they just said that they were heavy on both sides."

I said, "I wonder if I did the right thing. I could have got those men the hell out of there."

He replied, "You did what you were ordered to, didn't you?"

I answered, "Yes."

He said, "Then don't worry about it." I told him that it was eating away at me. I wanted to find out the casualties and if it were worth it. I wanted to know if I had done the right thing.

Dee came back in a couple of hours. She stayed until visiting hours were over. She said that they had decided to leave the next day, and that they hadn't decided on the time yet. When it came time for her to leave, the tears started to flow. I said, "Hey, wait a minute. I will see you tomorrow." I told her, "You have to make the best with what you've got and be thankful that you have that much." As she was leaving, I told her that I didn't want to see any tears tomorrow. She nodded her head. I knew tomorrow was going to be a rough day. When I got drafted, she cried the whole night before the day I was to leave. And the third day, I was at Fort Mead; her mother and brother brought her down that evening. Her mother told me that she had been crying since I'd left.

The next morning came early. She came over early and told me that they were leaving right after lunch. She was to be in front of the hospital at noon. We talked a lot of what life was going to be like after I got out. The time flew by, and before we knew it, it was time for her to leave. After a few hugs and kisses, I whispered in her ear, "Just straighten up and turn and walk away. It will be easier that way for both of us." She did just that, and after she was about two beds away, she looked back, and I winked at her and said, "I will be home before you know it." A very slight smile came over her face, and she nodded her head and walked away.

Two days later, I was allowed out of bed. A day or two later, I was allowed to go anywhere in a wheelchair. A few days after that, I didn't even need the wheelchair. I had the freedom of the hospital. That was as long as I was back when the medicine was due. In less than a week, the bandages came off my head. I needed a haircut at least on one side and back.

The vision in my right eye was blurred. An eye doctor was brought in for it. He had seen me every day for at least two weeks. With the medication he had me on, he got the vision down to twenty-forty in the right eye.

Then he gave me the bad news, a lot of it. He told me that the eye was permanently damaged, and that it would never be any better than it was then. He told me the only thing it could do was get worse. He said he was taking me off the medication to see if it would hold its own. Then came the low blow. He said if it did he was turning me back to the other doctor recommending me fit for duty. As far as the eye went, I thought I would get out.

By this time, my arm was out of the sling for some time. I had a letter off to the squad. I thought they should be getting it by now. I could just imagine them reading it and then yelling to everyone, "Hey, Beaver is gold bricking it at Walter Reed.

I asked everything. I wanted to know. I also asked how many of the squad were still there, and who the squad leader was now. I thought it might be Davis or maybe Castel.

The medical doctor that had me for my head and arm came in to see me a day after the eye doctor had given me the bad news. I asked about going back on duty. He said, "Let's just wait and see. As far as I can see, I think you're ready for some rest and rehabilitation." That meant home.

I asked, "How soon?"

He replied, "As soon as the eye doctor okays it." He told me that the doctor wanted to see what would happen after I was off the medication in a few days maybe.

As soon as he left, I broke my neck getting to a phone to call home and told Dee the good news. I also told her the bad news about the eye. She said to let her know a day or two ahead of time so they could come down for me. I asked them if they could find room to bring my mother with them. She liked to travel and would enjoy the trip. She said she would.

It was almost a week later when the doctor told me, "Guess what?"

I said, "I don't know. What?"

He told me that the eye doctor said I could go home.

He said, "But he would only agree to ten days, and then he wants to see you."

I asked, "When can I leave?"

He said, "As soon as they get your leave papers typed up. Probably this afternoon."

It was nearly lunch time when I went to the phone to call Dee. When I got her I asked, "Do you want me to get a bus, or do you want to come down and get me?"

She said, "Hold on for a minute." She got back, and I asked where she was. She said she went next door to call her brother at work. I told her I could get a bus and save them both the long trip. She said, "Stay where you are. We'll be there as soon as we can."

It was about a six-hour drive. I went back to one ward and got ready to go. Everyone was kidding me about it. It was quarter 'till four when the nurse brought my leave papers to me. She smiled and said, "Take it easy at first, and we'll see you in ten days." I hung around the ward waiting for them talking and carrying on with the guys.

Around eight o'clock in the evening, the crew arrived, and my mother was with them. After a hug from her and a kiss from Dee, I bid the guys in the ward farewell. I told them that I would see them in ten days. We left the hospital and stopped at the first restaurant we came to. I wasn't hungry, but they were starved. They hadn't eaten since they left that morning. I just had a cup of coffee.

It was a long drive home, but it seemed short to me. I was the center of attraction, and all the conversation was directed at me. We got home about 2:50 a.m. We stopped at Dee's home first, and after about half an hour, we decided we would stay at my house since my parents were the only ones there. They lived in a six-room house.

When we got there, my mother took me by the hand upstairs and into my dad's bedroom. I said, "Let him sleep. He has to go to work in the morning." She ignored me and shook him several times to wake him up. When he was awakened, I'll never forget the look on his face. His eyes lit up, and he smiled from ear to ear. He put his arms around me and patted me on the back. We sat on the side of the bed and talked for a while. I told him that he'd better get some sleep and that I would see him tomorrow.

The next day was Friday, and everyone was working. My mother, Dee, and I had quite a day. My car was jacked up on blocks in the garage. I got it running and down off the blocks. I took it and had it serviced. I got it an oil change, grease job, and everything else was checked. I was surprised that it ran good. Later, I found out that my father started it every week or two, and let it run for a few minutes.

When I arrived back home, everyone was there. My three brothers and my sister were all there. We had our evening meal and just sat around and talked. My oldest brother Harold was leaving for Georgia. He was taking his family to visit his wife's relations. He was leaving early in the morning. He wanted us to stay at his place and keep an eye on it. We agreed to it.

He lived on a small farm. It consisted of about thirty acres of land. It was a quiet and peaceful place, but we didn't get much time to ourselves. It seemed like someone was always coming or going. We were there for about four or five days. I was enjoying myself so much that I had almost forgotten about the army. One day, my small niece asked, "What's war like?" The expression on my face must have changed drastically. Her mother came and got her and started to scold her.

I said, "Don't do that. She was just curious." I then realized that all the time I'd been home, this was the first time anyone had mentioned the service.

That evening when Dee and I were alone; I told her that since I had been home, nobody had brought up the army or the war at all. I asked her if they were told to do it, or if it was just a thing that the family had decided on upon themselves. She told me that the family had just decided not to mention it. I thanked her for it, and that I had almost forgotten that I was still in the army. I was enjoying being home very much.

The time came soon for me to go back. Dee wanted to find someone to take me in my car. I told her it would be best if I just get a bus. When it was time, Dee and her brother drove me to Pittsburgh. I caught the bus, and eight hours later, I was in Walter Reed.

When I got back, there was a letter for me from the squad. They said that they were glad to hear from me, and they hoped I was doing good. They were glad to hear that I still had all my limbs and that I was still in one piece. Davis was the squad leader now. The whole squad was still together. They got a replacement for me, four or five days after I had left. They wrote that every hill since hill 427, they were advancing steadily. The enemy had been offering light resistance. They gave me the casualty report for hill 427. It was nineteen men dead and forty-two men wounded. They asked me to write when I could. The whole squad signed it, including the new man. We communicated several times after that. I raised Davis about being the squad leader and having to make all the decisions.

The next day, I went through the usual test and exams. Then I was off to see the eye doctor. After I was there for five days, the doctor came to see me. He said he was returning me to duty as soon as the eye doctor okayed it. I went to see the eye doctor that after noon and told him about it. He said that I could go right away. He called the other doctors and told them. He then told me that wherever I went that my records would follow me. The eye clinic there would want to see me.

I went to the ward and was only there a short time when the doctor came in to see me. He told me that my orders were being made out right away. He said I could probably leave in a few hours. He wished me good luck and started to leave. He then turned and said, "I managed to get you seven days delay in route. That was the best I could do." I jumped out of bed and thanked him. I started to pack and then thought that I should call Dee. I thought again and decided to walk in on her and surprise her.

I was ready to leave at four o'clock. I was saying my goodbyes, and one of the nurses told me that it was about time that I get home. Another man asked me, "Why don't you just get a hop?" They called the Andrews Airforce Base. I was in luck. They had a plane going to Pittsburgh and leaving at three thirty. They got me military transportation from the hospital. I just made it in time for the flight. The flight sergeant had just got done with orienting the passengers on what to do in case of an emergency. He turned and saw me boarding and said that I had to go through it all again. I said, "I am an airborne sergeant."

He picked up a parachute and handed it to me and said, "Then put this on. If you don't get out, nobody is getting out."

I was in Greater Pittsburgh airport at seven o'clock. I got to a phone and called Dee. When she got the phone, I asked, "Do you want to come and get me, or should I get a bus?" She was dumbstruck.

She asked, "Did you get another leave?"

I said, "No, just a delay in route."

She asked, "How long?"

I replied, "Seven days."

She said, "We will be there as soon as we can."

I asked, "Where are you going?"

She said, "Walter Reed."

I said, "I'm not there. I'm at the Greater Pittsburgh Airport." She told me that she'd be there in an hour.

I had an hour or a little better to kill. I didn't think that they'd make it in an hour. I browsed around the airport for an hour and then took my bags out to the parking lot to wait. It was a warm summer evening. I only had to wait about fifteen minutes when they pulled along beside me.

After several handshakes and kisses, we got in the car and started home. Dee, my mother, and I were in the backseat. We had just pulled out of the parking lot when Dee whispered, "Where to?"

I said, "Home."

She said, "No, after that."

I said, "Hell, I don't know. I never even looked to see." I got my orders out. I was to report to Fort Jackson, South Carolina, for assignment to the third army.

After another six wonderful days and nights at home, I left for Fort Jackson, South Carolina. I drove my own car down. The trip was uneventful.

I arrived in Fort Jackson and spent three days processing. On the fourth day, they asked where I wanted to go in the third army area. I asked, "What choice do I have?"

They said, "You're an airborne. You can go one of three places: Fort Benning, Georgia; Fort Campbell, Kentucky; or Fort Bragg, North Carolina." They left the choice to me. I picked Fort Bragg, North Carolina. The sergeant asked me why I had chosen Fort Bragg.

I said, "It's the closest one to home."

He said, "That's a good enough reason."

That afternoon, I got orders to report to Fort Bragg replacement company of the eighty-second airborne division. I got travel pay and had two days to report there.

I stayed at Jackson that night. I left after chow the next morning. I thought I would get there a day early and check out the post. When I arrived, I had to get a post license for my car, so I spent half the day doing that and then drove around the post for a while. Later on that day, I decided that I needed a place to sleep so I found the eighty-second replacement company and checked in.

The next day, I got assigned to the 504 airborne infantry regiment. When I arrived there, there was about fifteen of us reporting. I got assigned to (you guessed it) the Easy company second battalion.

It was after dark. Friday when I finally got there. I was assigned to weapons platoon sixty mortars. The sergeant in charge told me that I didn't have to worry about inspection the next morning. I was just to fall out in class A uniform and not worry about it.

The next morning, the inspection officer went up and down the ranks inspecting each man. When they got to me, the platoon sergeant just walked by me to the next man. The inspecting officer stopped in front of me. The platoon sergeant said that I had just arrived and didn't have time to get ready for inspection. He looked me up and down and went on to the next man. They inspected the barracks next. The same thing happened there. I wondered, "What kind of spit and polish outfit did I get into?" I soon found out. As soon as they got my records, I was made squad leader of the first squad of the fifty-seventh section. They trained daily; it was like basic training all over again. Every day, we were sent out to the field and ran into a different problem just like basic.

One day, we went out and ran a problem that reminded me of hill 427. After the problem was over, the lieutenant in charge held a class on it. After all the pros and cons were ironed out, the lieutenant in charge started to tell the class about a hill in Korea like this one. He told them that a non-commission officer was in charge of it. He told us that he had held the hill for over a day with overwhelming odds and then added that he had better than fifty percent casualties but stayed and denied the enemy use of that hill. He then said that this action probably saved the lives of hundreds of GIs. It also opened the door for a big push. He also told us that he had inflicted ten times as many or more casualties on the enemy as he had. He added, "Nobody knows why he stayed and fought against such odds, but he did. We're damn glad and lucky he did."

I was not sure that he was talking about hill 427, but I thought he was. I raised my hand, stood up, and said, "Sir, maybe nobody ever asked him why he stayed."

The lieutenant laughed and said, "I don't think that is the reason, but we don't know. Someone would have gotten around to it." I said no more and sat back down.

I don't think that I could have answered him anyway. I don't know why I stayed. It must have been the attitude of the men. The attitude I had gotten from them, from their actions, and conversations I had with them was, "No slanty-eyed SOB was going to push us off that hill."

I thought a lot about it on the march back. It made me feel a lot better about it. The lieutenant didn't know it, but he had answered all my questions about the hill. It eased my mind and seemed like a heavy load was finally off my shoulders.

I asked the platoon leader one day if they ever had any let up in the training. He explained that they were a combat-ready outfit. He told me that we were ready to strike anywhere in the world in twenty-four hours. He then told me that if any trouble were to break out that we would be the first ones to go. I thought, "Oh boy, what did I get myself into?"

By this time, my medical records had caught up to me. One morning at reveille, the first sergeant called my name. I answered him. He told me that I had an appointment at the eye clinic at zero nine hundred hours. That meant a day off. I didn't have to go to the field with the company. When I got to the eye clinic, they put me through the mill. When the doctor got done, he said, "You have a permanent eye injury, and it won't get any better." He said that he wanted to try a new drug on me for a while though. I received a bottle of pills that I had to take every four hours. I had to go to the eye clinic every other day Monday, Wednesday, and Friday. Each time there, I got a blood test to see how the drug was affecting me. After three weeks, they let me go. They told me if anything came up like pain or blurred vision, I was to get up there.

So it was back to the company for more training. It went on day after day. One day, we marched out for about three hours to a clearing in the pine woods. Then we got there, we were told to fall out and rest. A short time later, a chaplain pulled up in a jeep. Everyone started to moan. I asked what was going on. The sergeant in charge of the second squad told me, "All this way for a class on citizenship and morality."

The chaplain was a first lieutenant. He was of average height and thin. He was young in his mid-to late twenties. He had us form a half circle and started his class. He seemed very sincere as he tried to get his point across.

I forgot what he talked about. I was paying more attention to him. He soon gave us a break. He turned and went to his jeep which was parked behind him. I walked up behind him and said, "Excuse me, sir, do you have a moment?"

He turned and said, "I always have time for a troubled mind." When he turned, I saw he had the deepest blue eyes that seemed to look right into your mind. I just stared into his eyes for a moment.

I told him then what had happened on the bridge. I told him about having no control over my movement. I also told him that I had felt drawn to the bridge and about the chills and the bumps and the tingle in my fingers. I said, "My MI wouldn't fire, but it fired when we got fired upon. Sergeant Altman's weapon wouldn't fire at me either. I went to see the chaplain, and I just wasn't satisfied with his explanation."

When I was done telling him everything, he looked at me and smiled. He reached out and put his hand on my shoulder. When he did, I got the chills, the goose bumps, and the tingling in my fingers. He just said, "God is never there when we expect him, but he is never too late." I will never forget that.

I started to sob. I walked around the jeep to the pine woods. I leaned against a tree with my back to the company. The chaplain called the class to order. The lieutenant started to get them organized and started to yell at me. I heard the chaplain say, "Lieutenant, let that man alone. If anyone here doesn't need this, it's him."

After the chaplain's class was over, I went back to him. He smiled as he saw me coming up to him. I asked, "Did you feel anything, sir?" He just smiled harder and offered me his hand.

I shook it, and he said, "Good luck, trooper." I thanked him and took my place with my squad. All the way back, I kept thinking about the chaplain and his eyes. I also thought about his explanation. How simple and complete it was. The march back seemed to go very quickly.

When we got back and dismissed, I went into the barracks and sat on my foot locker for a while. I thought, "Here it is Mid-November. I have probably been here a little over three months. I have already made five training jumps, marched well over five hundred miles, and probably doubled time half that much. I only have about two months to go. I wonder if I will make it." I felt sorry for the men who were RA (regular army) with two or two and a half years to go.

I thought about home. I wondered if my dad and brothers were getting ready for deer season. I thought it would be nice to be there for just one hunt.

It hit me then. I must have had at least thirty days leave or more coming to me. I got up and went straight to the orderly room and told the first sergeant about my leave. I asked if I could have all of it starting December 1. He Just grinned and said I could put in for it. He told me that he didn't know if I would get all of it. He explained that over the holidays, most men want their leave time. He said, "They can't let all of them go, so they let half go for Christmas and half go for New Year's, but we will try and see what happens."

About two days before Thanksgiving, I asked the first sergeant about my leave. He said, "I just turned it in and haven't heard anything about it." He then added, "I think you have a good chance to get most if not all of it."

But as usual, this was not to be. The day after Thanksgiving, I awoke with a bad blood shot right eye and blurred vision. I went on sick call. The medic sent me to the eye clinic. Once I was there and examined, the doctor said, "I'm going to admit you. I want you here where I can keep an eye on you." I was admitted to the Fort Bragg army hospital where I was kept for seventeen days. I got out on December 15 with 20-40 vision in my right eye.

When I got back to the company, I asked the first sergeant about the leave. He told me that thirty-two days came through for me, but he had cancelled it. I asked what chances I had of getting some of it. He said, "I'll see what I can do. I don't know how much you can get because you're getting out on January 15." I asked him to see what he could do for me. Two days later, he told me that he had gotten me a twelve-day leave starting December 23.

I thanked him a whole lot for it. He just said, "Go and enjoy yourself. You deserve it." Training was lax, and we didn't do too much. About half the men were already on leave. On the twenty-second, just after noon chow, the first sergeant sent for me. When I got to the orderly room, he handed me my leave papers. He said, "You can take off now if you want to. I will cover for you." I thanked him and explained that I was driving and would rather do most of it late at night. I told him that I planned to leave at nine or ten that night. He said, "Suit yourself and have a good holiday." I thanked him again and said, "The same to you."

After the evening chow, I explained to the other squad leader what I planned to do. I told him that I was going back to the squad room to pack a few things that I was going to take. I asked him if he were going to be around at 9:00 to wake me up. He said he would.

I went and packed my bag and lay down. The next thing I knew, the other squad leader was awakening me. He told me that it was time to go. I got up and freshened up. I picked up my bag and started to leave. I wished the other two squad leaders, who were good friends, a happy holiday. They returned the feeling, and I walked out into the barracks. Turning to go out the side door. I wished the men in the barracks the same. I waved as I started for the door.

As I got to the door, the platoon sergeant was coming in. He said, "Are you leaving us now?"

I just said with a smile, "Yes, sergeant." He asked if I would mind if he walked me to my car. I wondered why because the car was a quarter mile away. I said, "No, sergeant, I don't mind. I would be glad to have the company." As we walked, he talked about the weather. He hoped I would have a white Christmas. He did most of the talking. I was still wondering what was up.

As we neared the car, he said, "Beaver, do you mind if I ask you a personal question?"

I said, "No, Sergeant, fire away."

He said. "Ever since we ran that problem about the hill, and we had class on it. I've wondered about you. Do you remember when they said, 'What made the sergeant in command stay and do what he did?' Do you remember what you did?"

I said, "Yes, I got up and said that maybe nobody had ever asked him."

He said, "I've looked over your records. You've got one hell of a war record. Yet 90 percent of the company doesn't even know you were ever over there. The sergeant we were talking about in the problem was you, wasn't it?"

I said, "I don't know. It could have been. As for the other part of your question I have no good memories of it, just bad ones." I have seen men die just about every way they can in war. I would just like to forget it and talking doesn't help one damn bit. (This is a practice I still have today. If anyone ever asked, I'd tell them that I had never left the country, and that I got hurt in war games in this country. When anyone who was ever there talks about it, I walk away from the conversation.)

He said, "The hill you got hit on. How bad was it?"

I said, "I took ninety-three men up there, and it was bad enough. We had nineteen dead and forty-two wounded."

He then said, "I hope there was no offense taken."

I said, "No, sergeant, you're just doing your job knowing your men. There was no offense offered and none taken."

He then said, "I have an occasional drink with the lieutenant in charge of that problem. I told him that I thought you were the sergeant in charge of that hill." He said if you were that, he owes you an apology.

I said, "Oh my, Sergeant, the lieutenant doesn't owe me an apology. He answered a lot of questions of mine that no one else could. Ever since that problem, life has been a little easier for me."

He then wished me a good time and a merry Christmas. I thanked him and wished him the same. He reached through the car window and patted me on the shoulder and said, "Drive carefully. I don't want to lose you now."

As I left the post, I looked at my watch and it was ten o'clock. I gassed up in Spring Lake and started north. I didn't call or write to Dee to tell her that I was coming home. I thought that I would just drop in on her. I hadn't wrote to her since I knew I had the leave about three days before.

As I headed the car north on route 15A through Virginia, I kept thinking of the talk I had with the sergeant. I wondered if I had done the right thing. I thought that when I got back everyone would be asking questions about it. I then thought, "Hell, I would only be there a week and then off to separation. I can put up with it that long."

As night wore into morning, I wondered if Dee would be surprised to see me, or if she was kind of expecting me. I got on the Pennsylvania turnpike about 8:30 a.m. and headed west to New Stanton and then north onto route 119. It was about 11:00 a.m. when I pulled up in front of Dee's house, I parked the car and walked up to the front door. I thought maybe she would answer it. I did, but her mother answered my knock. She said, "My god, what are you doing here?" She asked me why I had knocked.

I said, "I thought someone else might have answered it."

She said, "Wait here, I'll tell her that someone wants her at the door," She pushed the door nearly closed. I could hear her calling, "Dolores, someone wants you at the door."

I heard Dee say, "Who is it?"

Her mother answered, "One of your friends," A few seconds later the door opened, and Dee was standing there. Her eyes seemed to light up.

I said, "Your black eyes are sparkling." That was one of my nicknames for her. She has very dark brown eyes.

After our usual greetings, a few kisses and hard hugs, we went in. I had a dozen questions to answer. One of them was, "Have you had anything to eat yet?" The answer was, "No." Dee started to make me something to eat. While she did, I called home to tell my mother that I was back, and I would see her after I had got some sleep. It was close to noon. I told her to wake me in two hours. I went to sleep in her room just off the living room. I think I was asleep before I hit the bed. Dee awakened me at three o'clock. I got up and showered and changed. We decided to go to my home for supper. We called my parents and let them know that we were coming.

After we had supper and rested for a few hours, I asked Dee if she would like to go to town and mingle with the Christmas shoppers. She agreed, and we drove down town and parked the car. We started to walk on the avenue. It was crowded like all the stores were. We met a few of my friends who we chatted to for a few minutes. I turned to Dee and said, "I hope we run into a few of your friends. I want to pawn you off for a while so I can buy you a Christmas present."

She said, "Oh no, you don't. I've already got my Christmas present."

We both enjoyed this leave very much. We had very nice holidays. We visited with friends and relations daily. I met some of Dee's relations whom I had never met as Dee did some of mine.

Before we both knew it, it was time for me to go back. Early the morning of January 3, I got up and ready to go. Dee walked me to the car. I knew the good-byes were not going to be bad this time. In twelve days, I would be coming back a civilian. Dee didn't shed a tear as we said our good-bye. I looked over my shoulder, or as I pulled out, and I thought I almost saw her smile.

When I pulled onto the main highway and headed the car south, I thought of the long grueling drive ahead of me. It took a little over twelve hours to get there. That was with just two stops for fuel. I got back about 9:00 p.m. I signed in at the orderly room and went back to the barracks.

Everyone seemed glad to see me. After mingling in the barracks for a while, I went to the squad room and unpacked. The whole time I was thinking that soon I would be packing to go home for good.

The next day, it was raining. We stayed in and had classes on weapons. I noticed the squad was extra courteous to me. They did little things that they normally wouldn't do. I had one man in my squad who just hated authority. I think that no matter who had him, he would resent them. He was even being a model trooper. He did what he had to do without "griping" and even offered to help me set up a fifty-seven recoilless rifle. When he did, I just looked over to the platoon sergeant. He just shrugged his shoulders and smiled; I knew what it was. The platoon sergeant had told everyone about me when I was on leave.

The weather stayed bad. We even got some snow. The training schedule was made to suit the weather. I didn't mind it at all. On the seventh of January, I was notified to report to the separation center on the main post. The next morning after chow, I once again moved out bag and baggage. I said my good-byes with a promise to stop back before I left.

I arrived at the separation center, and it was just like the introduction center. After five days of running all over the place, we were in a class of about two hundred. They talked to us for about hour or so, giving us our rights and benefits. They painted a rosy picture for anyone who wanted to re-enlist. They then asked if anyone wanted to file claim against the government. I raised my hand. There were four of us who did, and we were told to go to a certain room.

They told everyone they could go then except for the airborne men. There were about fifty of us. A man from a parachute manufacturing company offered us jobs. The jobs consisted of testing new chutes. Another man offered us jobs that jumping was involved in also. They both paid quite well.

I then went to file claim against the government. I got there as they were finishing up with the other men. They explained everything to me and also told me that it would detain me two days longer.

I was separated on the seventeenth of January 1955 early in the morning. I thought of getting in my car and going straight home. It would get me there about midnight. I thought about the promise I had made to my friends back in the company. I thought it wouldn't take too long to go back and see them for the last time.

I drove down to the company and got there about 10:00 a.m. Some of the men were there, but most were out training. I decided to wait for noon chow when everyone would be there.

The company got in about 11:00 a.m., and I visited with them until about 11:30 a.m. I told them that I was going to take off, but they wouldn't let me go. I had to stay and have noon chow with them.

After chow, about five or six of them walked me to my car. After a handshake with them and well-wishing both ways, I jumped in my car and headed it north.

6

AFTER ABOUT FOUR OR FIVE hours on the road, I needed food and fuel. I decided to stop somewhere where I could grab a quick meal. I thought, "I'm in no hurry now. I've got my whole life ahead of me and no certain schedule to keep."

I found a gas station with a restaurant next to it. I gassed up and pulled in front of the restaurant. I went in and ate a quick meal. As I was leaving, I bought a pack of cigarettes. I don't know why. I just bought them.

After about another hour on the road, I looked down at the cigarettes. I picked up the pack and opened them. I took one out and looked at it. I pushed in the cigarette lighter and waited for to get hot. It popped out, and I took it and started to light the cigarette. As I did, I thought of a cigarette lighter I once had. How nice it would be if I still had it. I would put it in a velvet-lined watch case and framed it. I thought I would never use it just keep it for the rest of my life. But I didn't have it. I lost it on hill 427. I lost everything I had. I left there with only the clothes that were left on me, and I didn't keep them for very long. I have been smoking from that day on.

After I got home, I ran around and visited friends and relatives. I got my old job back. Dee and I set up housekeeping in a three-room apartment.

Things went pretty normal for us. About a month after I got out, I got a letter to go to the veteran's administration in Pittsburgh.

I went to Pittsburgh on that date and time. They gave me a complete physical exam; I then returned home and several weeks later, I got a letter from them. They said that my right eye condition was service connected but didn't disable me enough to award a claim.

The first few years of young married life went normal for Dee and I. I was working every day. We bought a new car and furniture.

On March 7, 1956, Colleen Lynn, the first of our seven children was born. She was a healthy eight-pound-and nine-ounce baby. She completely changed our lives. The running and visiting and going here and there were out. We stayed home much more now.

In early September, my right eye flared up again. I wrote to the veteran's administration. While waiting to hear from them, my eye got worse. It got so blood shot; it looked. like a pool of blood. It got very painful. I was blind in it. I sat up many nights with aspirin and cold towels on my head.

One day at work, a co-worker suggested that I go to see a layout man who worked very near to us. He explained that he was the commander of the local VFW.

I walked over to him and explained everything to him. He just stared at my eye the whole time. Tears just poured right out of it; when I finished telling him my story, he gave me a paper and pen and asked me to write my name, address, phone number, and VA claims number on it. He said he would turn it over to his service officer and get him moving on it.

At dinner time, he came back to me and said that he would make some phone calls. He told me he wanted me to go down to the veteran's administration hospital on University Drive in Oakland, Pittsburgh, for treatment. He said if its service is connected, they will have to look at me. He suggested I go early the next morning.

The couple who lived in the apartment above us were good friends of ours. His name was Bill. He worked third shift in the same plant of ours. He was also a volunteer ambulance driver. He volunteered to drive me down. We planned to leave shortly after he got home from work.

The next day was October 2. We left at about seven forty-five. After all the questions and forms were filled out, I was finally sent to the eye clinic. When I got there, there were about ten or twelve people ahead of me. A clerk took my paper work and told me to have a seat.

I thought I was in for another hour or two of waiting, when a doctor walked in the waiting room. He stood in the middle of the room and called a name. As he did, he looked over all of us like he was wondering which one of us he was getting. When he looked at me he walked right over to me. He looked me in the eye and asked my name. He then told me to go to a certain room in the clinic.

I went back to the room. Several minutes later, he came in. After all his questions and a good look in the eye, he left and came back with two other doctors. They all had a good look and started to discuss it among themselves.

After they were through, the first doctor came back to me. He started to put drops in it every ten or fifteen minutes. I found out he was trying to dilate it. After three or four tries with the drops, I thought he was giving up on it.

He took me to another room. I saw Bill on the way there. He was all alone. I told him that he should go get something to eat. The doctor asked if he was waiting for me. Bill said he was. The doctor told him to go home because he was keeping me. Bill left, and the doctor and I walked into another room.

He got a hypodermic needle ready for a shot. He turned to me, and I was going to ask, "Arm or hip?" Before I could, he said, "Open it wide and don't move." He held the eye open and gave me the shot directly in the eye ball. When he depressed the plunger, I could feel and taste the fluid going down my nose and throat. It didn't work. The eye still didn't dilate, and it hasn't until this day.

I was admitted to the hospital October 2, 1956. After trying several things on me that didn't work, they put me on a new medication. I was on it for about two weeks without any improvement. Taking my eye out was mentioned several times. One of the doctors was against it. After about two more weeks on the medication without any results, the doctors were starting to get serious about taking my eye.

Then there was a marked improvement on it. I could see a little out of it. I could count fingers at several feet. They doubled my medication and put me on a salt free diet. My food was weighed, and I was also weighed every day. They took a blood test every other day to see how the medication was affecting me.

After about a month of this without much more improvement, the doctor came into my room. He told me they were going to try typhoid fever shots on me. He explained that they would inject a controlled amount of typhoid germs in me. That would give me typhoid fever for a controlled amount of time.

Before he left, I told him that sometimes my body would quiver all over. He just said that it was hunger tantrums and left. He told me if I got them again, I was to tell the nurse. She would give me a shot.

On Monday, they started the typhoid shots. They were bad. It was just like having typhoid fever for twenty-four hours. I got the shot every other day for about two weeks. I was improving. As the matter of fact, I was coming along so good that they started to give two or three other guys in the ward the same treatment. They all blamed me for getting it.

The doctor came in on Sunday. I said to him, "Oh no, not on Sunday."

He said, "Not you, these other ones." He told me my temperature only went up one degree with the last shot. He then told me that he had given me all the law allowed him to. Then he said, "You've got one hell of an immunity against typhoid. You will never get that and that's a promise."

Dee came to see me every day. I told her that she didn't have to. It must have been hard for her getting a babysitter and driving thirty miles one way every day. But she still came. Snow, rain, or shine, she was there.

One day in Mid-December, she came early in the evening. After being there for a few minutes, she told me that there was something down in the lobby that she wanted me to see. I told her that it was almost time for a pill. As soon as I got it, we would go down; it wasn't long until the nurse brought it, and we started down.

When we got there, Dee's girlfriend was sitting on a couch with Colleen. She was just past nine months old. I hadn't seen her for more than two months. We walked across the lobby to where they were. Then we got a few steps away. Dee stopped me and said, "Call her." I knelt down and called her. She walked over to me. Colleen was walking.

They kept the medication up until late January. Finally, the doctors decided that the eye wasn't going to get any better. The vision was either 3-200 or 2-300. I don't remember. They decided to decrease the medication slowly.

By February twelfth, they had it down to one pill every four hours. They discharged me four months and two weeks after I was admitted. I was an outpatient. I had to go back every other day for about a month. Then it went down to once a week. I was finally able to return to work. I went back less and less all the time until finally six months later, I was completely discharged.

On April 3, 1957, Dee gave birth to Jeffery Allen. He was the second of our seven children. On October 7, 1959, Donald Paul was born. Then on December 1, 1960, Gregory Mark was born.

We then decided that we had better invest in a home of our own. We bought an older two-story home in our old hometown. Everything went smoothly for several years. On March 25, 1962, Clayton Harry was born. He was the fifth of our seven children. Then in the spring of 1965, Dee was pregnant with our sixth child.

One day, we visited some friends who lived in a second floor apartment. I thought I had heard some kids arguing in the back-yard, and I walked out onto the back second floor porch to check. I could see no children in the backyard. I walked over to the side of the porch to look alongside the house. As I was walking, the porch collapsed. I threw myself outward to clear the side walk and steps leading onto the first floor porch. As I did, I was getting my body in position to make a PLF (parachute landing fall). It didn't work. I hit a wire clothes line which I sprung off of like a spring board. I hit the ground hard.

I had fallen about eighteen feet. I couldn't move. I was lying face down. I got turned so I could holler for them to close the door before one of the kids walked out. When I did, I saw Colleen already lying on the sidewalk behind me.

I tried to yell, but I couldn't talk above a whisper. I must have had the wind knocked out of me pretty good. They were alerted to what had happened inside by a neighbor. I looked as Colleen lying on the sidewalk. She was lying there like a wet rag. I called to her several times, but she didn't answer or even move.

Help got to us. I told them not to move Colleen. They wanted to move me to a more comfortable position, but I wouldn't let them.

The ambulance finally arrived. They worked on Colleen first. They got her loaded and came for me. I told them I felt like I was busted up pretty badly. They strapped me on a board and got me loaded into the ambulance.

We arrived at the hospital, and both of us were worked on right away. They wheeled Colleen out and down the hall. She still hadn't regained consciousness yet. That was the last time I saw her for some time.

After putting me through the mill, they found I had a fractured vertebra, the third one above the tail bone, some lacerations, badly bruised hips, and some broken ribs.

I kept asking about Colleen, but I couldn't get any answers. It worried me. I thought that if she was alright they would have told me. The next day, when the doctor came in, I asked him about her. I found out she had a cerebral concussion and a broken collar bone.

After a few weeks in the hospital, we were both discharged the same day. I was in a brace and Colleen had some kind of harness to hold her shoulder back.

On August 17, 1964, which was our twelfth wedding anniversary, Gary Lee was born. He was our sixth child.

I was off work for nearly a year. We lost our home, car, and furniture. We were on welfare. We got some furniture from friends and relatives and decided to rent a house. Things were pretty rough. I kept bugging the doctor, asking when I could return to work. Before he could okay it, I got a letter from the plant telling me that I had been laid off.

Not long after that, the doctor told me to find a desk job. He told me that I would never be able to carry heavy work again. I shopped around for one. I found two of them, but neither paid much. It wasn't enough to support my family with.

I looked around some more and finally found a small machine and fabrication shop. I got hired as a milling machine operator.

The job didn't pay as much as my other one, but with the overtime involved, I was bringing home more.

The plant was a small one. It was divided into three departments. There were the small machine shop, the large machine shop, and the weld or fabrication shop. It had about forty men working two shifts. On my second day there, I decided to look the plant over. Most of my experience was in fabrication. I wanted to see their fabrication shop. To get to it, I had to go through the large machine shop. As I went into the large machine shop, the first person I saw was a man in his early to mid-twenties. He was about the same height and weight as Sergeant Altman. His color of hair and his eyes were the same. His build and facial structure were the same. His resemblance to Sergeant Altman was remarkable.

I just froze and stared at him. Through the haze of my half-dazed mind, I could make out the structure of the bridge as I did on that night in the moonlight. I could see the silhouette of a lonely soldier standing on the far end. I could feel the fear shot through my body like electricity. I could feel the grip of the MI rifle in my hands. I even felt the sweat rolled down my face, when I heard, "Is that you, Beaver?"

I don't know how long I stared at this man, but he was beginning to look strangely back to me. I regained my senses and quickly returned to the small machine shop. I started to ask questions about him. I asked one or two questions there. Not enough to arouse any suspicion. You can imagine the feeling that I had and the look on my face when I found out that his name was Altman. I concluded from the answers I got that he could not be closely related to Sergeant Altman. They must have been distant relatives. I doubt if he even knew that Sergeant Altman even existed.

I totally avoided this man. He must have thought that I didn't care for him. This was not so. He seemed like a very likable person. It was just that he awoke a sleeping giant within me. Should this book ever get published, and Jack reads it. I hope that he will forgive me. He no longer works with me. He quit several years ago to take a better job. I have lost all track of him.

Then once again, over a period of time in my mind, I was able to put the memories of Sergeant Altman back in its dormant stage.

After a month or so with everything going all right, I decided to visit the plant where I had been laid off from. I wanted to see what chances I had of being recalled. They told me that with my eye and now my back, the only thing they would be able to give me was a broom. I politely told him what he could do with his broom and left.

I went back to the small plant. About a year after I got hired, I moved into the fabrication shop where I am to this day. I have never been laid off.

After moving into the fabrication shop, I became a welder. On several occasions, I had to weld on Jack's machine. I would talk with him. Several times, I think I told him that I was in the army with a man with a name like his. I never told him that he would have passed for his twin brother. Looking at him was like looking at Sergeant Altman twelve years ago. He always answered the same thing each time I mentioned it: "Hell, we're like bad weeds. You will find Altman anywhere."

Several times, I had to weld on the machine next to his and would find myself staring at him. I don't think I saw him so often. I would always be walking up the hill talking to Sergeant Altman or be right on the bridge with him. Sometimes, I would be in the company command post looking down at his pleading eyes. He caught me several times. He must have thought that I was some kind of screw ball.

On October 29, 1965, Dee gave birth to Paula Diana. She was the last of our seven children. We had five boys and two girls.

Everything went normally for the next nine years. In the spring of 1974, Dee started to complain of getting dizzy spells. She complained periodically about them. She said that sometimes she thought that she was going to pass out. I coaxed her to see a doctor, but she wouldn't.

One day, when I returned home from work, there was an ambulance in front of our house. I ran into the house. It was Dee. She had had a seizure. Another ambulance had already taken her to the hospital.

She was there for one week. They ran all kinds of tests on her but could find nothing and released her.

On August 17, 1974, Colleen was married to Donald Lee Bosley. I got him a job in the same plant where I worked. They got an apartment in the same neighborhood. We saw a lot of them.

In March of 1975, my right eye acted up again. I was admitted to the veteran administrator hospital. I was totally blind in it. It looked bad. I was there for one week. The eye didn't respond to any of the treatment. The doctors decided that an operation may be necessary. They were going to freeze it. It was on Friday that the doctor came in to describe the operation to me. He told me what they were going to do and how. He told me that it would be done the first thing on Monday morning.

On Saturday, the reverend of the church, we went to regularly, came in to see me. He visited for nearly a half an hour and got ready to leave. Then he was leaving, I asked him if he would mind praying for me. He took me by the right wrist and prayed for several minutes. While he was praying, I got the same feeling as I had on the bridge, but I didn't associate it with the bridge at that time. He wished me well and left.

The next day was Sunday. Around noon, the doctor came in to see me. I said, "What are you doing here on Sunday? Did you come to build the patient's confidence?"

He said, "Yes, that as well as the doctors." He kept staring at my eye as he explained that he had never done this kind of operation before. He told me not to worry that there would be a team of doctors there that had done it many times.

He then said, "Let's take a walk up to the eye clinic. I want to take another look in there." He walked up the stairs one floor above the ward to the eye clinic. We were in the clinic for about a half hour. He gave my eye a good examination. He then walked me back to the ward. When we got there, he patted me on the back and said, "I will see you tomorrow."

That evening, I was walking the halls, when an orderly came by with a cart of juices, milk, and cookies. He asked if I would care for anything. I told him no because I wasn't allowed. I told him that I had an operation the next morning. A nurse was standing there and said, "You can have all you want. The operation has been cancelled."

The next day, when the doctor came in to see me, I asked him what happened to the operation. He said, "I have never seen so much improvement in one day as I have in you. I don't understand it, but if you stay as good as you are now, I will let you go home on Friday."

I didn't think too much about it until Wednesday when the same reverend came in to see me. We talked for a while. He said, "We said a prayer in church for you on Sunday." After he said that, it hit me. The feeling I had Saturday when he prayed for me was the same one I had on the bridge. I just paused for a moment thinking about it. I wondered why I didn't associate it with the bridge on Saturday. I thought that it was as plain as day, and I should have. I said, "It must have done some good reverend. They cancelled the operation."

He said, "I was going to ask you about that. You don't have any bandage or patch on it."

He left after about an hour of visiting. I kept wondering why I hadn't recognized the feeling immediately. It bothered me. I thought surely I couldn't be forgetting it. I would never do that. Then I thought about what the chaplain at Fort Bragg said. As I thought about it, I could see his deep blue eyes. He said, "God is never there when we expect him, but he is never too late."

I was discharged Friday as an outpatient. I was blind in the eye, but the eye was considered healthy. I am still an outpatient there five years later. It looks like I will be for a long time. I go in every four to six months for a checkup.

Everything went as well as could be expected for the next few years. Dee took her seizures once in a while but still refused to go to a doctor. I took her to the hospital a few times, but they treated her in the emergency room and let her go.

In the fall of 1977, I bought a lot. It was in the country near route 22 about thirty miles east of Pittsburgh. In the spring of 1978, we started to build a three-bedroom ranch house on it. The boys, my son-in-law, and I built it. We moved into the house in October of '78, and that is where we are today.

On June 24, 1973, Donald got married to Pamela Darleen Prinky. On August 19, 1973, Jeff got married to Kimberly Elizabeth

Mallet. We have three married children, and all have blessed us with granddaughters.

In the Spring of 1979, Dee took a very bad seizure. It happened early one morning when I was at work. Colleen called and told me that Dee was bad. She took one and fell out of bed. She hit her head on the nightstand and broke her nose. She got two beautiful black eyes from it.

I got home, and Colleen's husband Donny and I got her to the hospital. I remember signing her in. She looked like she was beaten or was in one hell of a fight. I thought that the first thing they were going to think was a domestic argument. Everyone at the hospital that asked were told that I was at work while this happened.

She took several seizures right after we got her there. I thought that the best thing that could happen to her. Every time I had taken her, she had never had one at the hospital before. I had to explain what she did and how she acted. This time they saw for themselves. They kept her about four days. After all the testing, we still knew nothing.

On Sunday night, Colleen and I were returning home from visiting her at the hospital which was about ten miles away from home when Colleen said, "There must be something wrong with her, or they would have told us by now." I thought for a moment. She could be right.

I then prayed that we would find out what was wrong. I asked God to let it be something they can cure or hold in check. I asked, "Please don't let it be cancer." I immediately got chills running up and down my back. The hair on my head felt like it was standing up. My fingers tingled and my forehead got wet with perspiration. I said nothing the rest of the way home.

When we got home, Colleen and some of the other kids were talking in the living room about their mother. They were all expressing their fears about what could be wrong with their mother.

I told them to stop it. I didn't want to hear that kind of talk. I said, "Your mother is going to be all right. I'm sure of it." With that, I said no more. I went straight to bed.

Monday, after work and supper, Colleen and I went straight to the hospital. All the way there, Colleen was wondering what they found out today. We got to the hospital and saw Dee. We got the same old news, nothing. Tuesday, we went back. This day was more productive. We found out that the doctor wanted a conference with Dee and I the next day.

Wednesday, I got up and called into work and told them I couldn't make it. I got the kids off to school. Colleen came over, and I asked her to go with me. We got to the hospital early. We sat there and talked; nothing was said about the upcoming conference. A few times, someone would say, "I wonder when the doctor is coming in?"

The doctor came right after lunch. He took us to a patient lounge and closed the doors. Then we were all seated; he looked at Dee and said, "Young lady, you've been a mystery to us for five years, but you no longer are." He then said with no pause, "You have a brain tumor."

He could have hit me with a sledge hammer. Could I have been wrong these years? Could all those times just have been coincidence? The doctor went on and explained the tumor. He said, "The brain is divided into two parts with a cushion like substance between them to keep them from banging into each other. Your tumor is on one cushion." He then paused and said, "It is definitely non-malignant. With today's new methods of testing and new equipment, it shows up quite clear. Comparing your old test when we know what we are looking for. It showed up as a shadow on them. Comparing the two tests it has not changed in size or shape in any way in five years. He then said that he had called in several neuro surgeons to look at them. They all agreed to leave it alone." Then he added, "As for the seizures, we can control them with medication now that we know what we have."

I thought right on again. How could I have doubted it. The doctor gave us a prescription to get. He then signed Dee's release. He then said, "If she has more than three seizures in a six-month period of time then I want to see her. If she doesn't, I want her in here every six months for tests. I want to make sure it stays quiet."

A few days later, I think it was Sunday. Colleen was joking with her mother in our kitchen about what all the kids had thought might be wrong with her. I was sitting there listening to them. When the conversation reached its peak, I spoke up and said, "I told you Sunday right that she was going to be all right."

Colleen turned and said, "That's right. How did you know?"

I came back with the title of a song that I think Tom T. Hall had out a few years ago. "Me and Jesus Got a Good Thing Going," with that I left the room.

It's been about a year since Dee's hospital stay. She is running about normal. She is averaging about three seizures per six months. She is on medication probably for the rest of her life as I am on mine for the rest of my life.

I have five boys who are of draft age, or nearly draft age, and I pray to God they will never have to go. If their country should call, I'm sure they will answer that call. I'm sure they wouldn't go running to Canada with their tails between their legs. I pray that no young man will ever have to go into battle again, for who really reaps the harvest of war?

7

DEE ONCE SAID TO ME jokingly that she was thinking of suing the United States government. I smiled at her and asked, "Why?" She said that she would rather have the carefree, happy-go-lucky guy that got drafted over the quite shy one she got back.

For it is the scars of battle that you cannot see that are the hardest and take the longest time to heal. Sometimes when I go to bed at night and close my eyes, I can still see that smiling oriental face through the sights of the MI rifle. Sometimes I can see the enemy medic kneeling down over me as our eyes met. Sometimes I can see the face of the enemy major in the light of my lighter, and sometimes I can see shells bursting then hear the anguished screams of the wounded and the dying. Once again I ask, "Who really reaps the harvest of war?"

We have four children at home yet. The oldest is nineteen, and the youngest is fourteen. They are not the best, but they are far from the worst. None of our seven children ever gave us any real trouble. Greg, the oldest one at home, likes country music. He has a few tapes of it. On one of them, he has Kris Kristofferson's, "Why Me Lord." When I hear it, I always say, "Yeah, why me?"

I don't know what he has in store for me. As life goes by one day at a time, there's one thing I do know: Whatever I try to do or wherever I go down life's winding road, I will never walk alone.

9 781640 969308